# Natural Babycare

A comprehensive guide to raising a child
in a natural, healthy and safe environment

JULIA GOODWIN

EBURY PRESS
LONDON

*To Simon, who held the fort brilliantly!*

1  3  5  7  9  10  8  6  4  2

Text copyright © Julia Goodwin 1997
Illustrations © Nicola Smee 1997

First published in the United Kingdom in 1997 by Ebury Press
Random House · 20 Vauxhall Bridge Road · London SW1V 2SA

Random House Australia (Pty) Limited
20 Alfred Street, Milsons Point, Sydney · New South Wales 2061 · Australia

Random House New Zealand Limited
18 Poland Road, Glenfield · Auckland 10 · New Zealand

Random House South Africa (Pty) Limited
Endulini, 5A Jubilee Road · Parktown 2193 · South Africa

Random House UK Limited Reg. No. 954009

A CIP catalogue for this book is available from the British Library

ISBN: 0 09 185333 8

Designed by Lovelock & Co.

Printed and bound in Portugal by Printer Portuguesa l.d.a

# Contents

ACKNOWLEDGEMENTS

I would like to thank Friends of the Earth, the London Food Commission and the Women's Environmental Network for their information. I would like to acknowledge *The Parents' Green Guide* by Brigid McConville (Pandora) for the help it provided. I would also like to thank Ione Brown, who helped me enormously with the research on Chapter Four and Karen Heavey, who did likewise on Chapters Two and Three. Finally, thanks to Dr Sue Bower for her comments on the manuscript.

# Introduction

If you've just had, or are about to have, a baby – congratulations. You are embarking on an exciting journey that will last for the rest of your life. The fun and satisfaction are impossible to describe until you experience them, but the responsibility can be awesome.

Every day we, as parents, are bombarded with news and advice. It sometimes seems that all the blame for children with health or behavioural problems is heaped at our door and yet, if our kids turn out to be normal, happy and healthy, it is despite all the bad things we have subjected them to!

Today's parents have access to more information than any other generation responsible for bringing up children. But all that knowledge – from books, magazines, TV and radio programmes and Internet sites – can be overwhelming. If we were to read every piece of relevant information on bringing up children, there would be no time left to actually do it.

Environmental organisations produce tomes of evidence about food and water pollution, air pollutants and lead poisoning. It makes gloomy reading. On the other hand, there is a lot of evidence to show that our children are growing bigger and stronger with each generation, so things can't be that bad.

In *Natural Babycare* I have tried to cover all the important issues likely to be encountered during your baby's day and later on in his childhood. These range from how to avoid food additives to safe bathing and natural remedies for minor ailments.

More generally, this book shows you how to make your home a healthier place with tips on natural furnishings, avoiding indoor pollutants and alerting you to possible danger zones round the house. Outdoor life, together with advice on coping with insect and animal bites, advice on pest control and sun protection, is covered too.

I have tried to paint a balanced picture, offering reasonable suggestions on ways to bring up children as naturally as possible in an increasingly artificial environment. However, we can take advantage of technological advances. Washing machines, dishwashers, the range of modern foods and health products now widely available have freed parents, particularly mothers, from much of the sheer, back-breaking drudgery of caring for babies and small children that our parents and grandparents endured.

Easy-wash, easy-care children's clothes, disposable nappies, convenience babyfoods and formula milk have each made life easier for many parents. But we now know more about the possible disadvantages of some of these products than we did 10 or 20 years ago. There is also a multi-million-pound baby market devising advertising campaigns to persuade us that our baby needs all these things and more. The truth is – he doesn't.

Be aware of the tremendous power of baby advertising and the way it is placed in publications you trust to give you honest information on babycare. Don't be sucked in by it. If you don't want a frilly cot bumper, don't buy it. If you feel a rucksack and a convertible pushchair will be the best way of transporting your baby, don't splash out on a luxury pram as well.

Make the best decisions you can in the light of the information you have. Don't give yourself a hard time if he has a jar of baby food twice a week or you've used a bathtime product that has given him a skin rash.

There is no such thing as a perfect parent – and who would want to have one if there were? Your baby will love you more than any other person in the world however many mistakes you make. Enjoy bringing him up and getting to know him.

NB I have referred to your baby as 'he' throughout this book. It was done purely to make it easier for you to avoid confusion about whether I am referring to the baby or the mother.

# CHAPTER ONE

# Feeding Your Baby

We are what we eat. The way you choose to feed your baby will undoubtedly influence not only his own adult eating habits but also his long-term health. Babies who enjoy varied diets with plenty of fresh foods will grow accustomed to these flavours. On the other hand, babies reared largely on processed and synthetic foods will have taste buds geared towards artificial tastes and textures.

We know that too many of today's teenagers consume convenience foods and fizzy drinks in large quantities. Indeed, a recent study highlighted the fact that most British children only consume the recommended amount of fresh fruit and vegetables on Christmas Day! By getting your baby into good eating habits early on you will make it easier for him to choose healthy alternatives as he grows up, such as baked potatoes instead of chips, salad instead of tinned vegetables and fruit juice instead of pop. His health will benefit, too. A recent survey of 5,000 British children revealed that ten-year-old boys are 17 per cent fatter and ten-year-old girls are six per cent fatter than they were twenty years ago. If this trend continues at the same pace, by the year 2050 the average ten-year-old will be as heavy as a full-grown adult, with the boys weighing 59 kg (9 st 4lbs) and girls weighing 57 kg (9 st). Heart disease, cancer and, for girls, osteoporosis, are all linked to diet. Getting your baby into good eating habits will give him the best possible start in life.

# Breastfeeding

Women have been breastfeeding babies for millions of years. All the research shows that it is the safest and healthiest way to feed a baby. As well as requiring no preparation, breastmilk's unique make-up can never be copied in formula milks.

Although breastfeeding is completely natural, it is a technique that has to be learned. Many women are tempted to give up if they experience difficulties. In the UK two-thirds of mothers breastfeed their babies to begin with but, by the age of four months, three-quarters of them are being bottlefed.

Not being able to see the amount of milk your baby is taking can lead to anxiety about whether he is 'getting enough'. Mothers need a lot of support and encouragement during the first six weeks when breastfeeding is becoming established and to do it successfully you really do need to make it your number one priority. You have to shut your eyes to the housework and concentrate on resting and eating well to build up your energy and your milk supply. That can be very difficult if you are coping alone, particularly if you have other small children who are also demanding your time and attention.

If you do persevere you will be rewarded with the knowledge that your baby is getting the very best start in life. You will also grow to really enjoy feeding him and to experience great satisfaction in the knowledge that you are providing everything he needs to grow and develop from within your own body.

### WHY BREAST IS BEST FOR YOUR BABY

A breastfed baby is protected against:

- Infection. Proteins in breastmilk called immunoglobulins or antibodies help to fight the bacteria that cause infections such as respiratory and urinary infections, glue ear and stomach upsets (gastroenteritis). In the UK it has been estimated that the Government would save £35 million each year on reduced hospital admissions for gastroenteritis if all babies were breastfed. Protection against infection can continue for at least two years after breastfeeding stops.

- Cot death. Statistics show that breastfed babies are far less likely to be victims of cot death (or sudden infant death syndrome), the biggest killer of children during the first year of life.

- Allergies. Eczema and asthma are far more common in bottlefed babies.

- Constipation. Breastfed babies' stools contain more water, making hard motions less likely.

- Obesity. Breastmilk is perfectly tailored to your baby's needs, so he is less likely to overfeed.

- Diabetes and childhood cancers. There is a lower incidence of these conditions among breastfed babies.

- Dental problems. Breastfed babies have shown to have less dental decay when they are older, due to incorrect positioning of teeth in the jaw.

- Low intelligence. Premature babies fed breastmilk were found to be more intelligent at 8 years old. Further research, however, has linked this to the mother's IQ level – the higher the IQ, the more likely she is to breastfeed. Mother's milk contains decosahexaenoic acid (DHA) which aids the rapid brain development that occurs during babyhood.

- Mental illness. One study showed that seven out of ten schizophrenic patients had been bottlefed. Some experts believe that the disease has only gained a foothold since mothers switched to bottlefeeding.

- Nitrate pollution. Nitrates, which affect a baby's ability to use oxygen properly, do not seem to pass into breastmilk although they are present in the tap water used to make up formula feeds.

### WHY BREAST IS BEST FOR YOU
If you breastfeed you are more likely to:

- be protected against osteoporosis, ovarian cancer and early breast cancer.

- lose weight without dieting (although some women find they hang on to a small fat reserve of an extra 3 kg (7 lbs) or so until they finish breastfeeding).

- be protected against pregnancy. High levels of prolactin help to block ovulation, although you should still use contraception if you want to avoid pregnancy.

- save time. Breastmilk arrives at the right temperature, ready for your baby to feed, and there is no time-consuming sterilising of bottles and teats to be done.

- save money. Breastfeeding costs nothing, although you will need to make sure you eat a healthy and balanced diet. Bottlefeeding a baby for six months costs over £200. If every baby born in the UK was bottlefed for six months, it would cost over £145 million.

- help protect the environment. The baby milk market uses 2,050,000 kg of steel each year to produce formula milk containers. Chlorine, which is used in the manufacture of plastic baby bottles, plays a major role in our most pressing environmental problem – the depletion of the ozone layer, global warming and acid rain. (See Breastfeeding and the environment on page 17.)

(See Breastfeeding and the environment on page 17.)

### THE FIRST MILK

As soon as possible after your baby is born you should put him to the breast. This is when his sucking reflex is strongest and the

### BENEFITS OF BREASTMILK

Human breastmilk is made up of water, proteins, carbohydrates, minerals, vitamins, hormones and enzymes like any other milk. But it is the unique combination of these substances which makes it the best, most natural source of nutrition for your baby. Here are some of the components which make it so special:

- Protein (lactoferrin). The low protein content of breastmilk is suited to a baby's immature kidneys. Formula milks have a higher concentration of protein.

  Lactoferrin also helps your baby to absorb iron and it stops bacteria from developing in the bowel.

- Casein. When milk enters a baby's stomach it is turned into curds and whey. The curds made from the milk protein casein pass more easily through the baby's digestive system than bulky formula curds.

- Cholesterol. Breastmilk contains cholestrol, which plays an important part in the development of the nervous system. It is also thought that exposing a baby to cholesterol early on reduces the harmful effects later on.

- Fatty acids (or longchain polyunsaturated fatty acids (LCP)). These help a baby's brain to develop and are not present in many formula milks.

- Interferon. This factor, which is passed into breastmilk directly from the mother, helps your baby to fight viral infections.

stimulation of your breast will help to promote a good milk supply. For the first two days your breasts will produce colostrum, a thick, creamy substance that is rich in antibodies. Even if you only feed your baby for a few days, the colostrum will help protect him against infection.

Colostrum is a high-density, low-volume feed. Your baby needs only a small quantity. It contains more protein and fat-soluble vitamins than mature breastmilk, but less fat, carbohydrate and water-soluble vitamins. It also has more cholesterol than mature milk.

### WHEN THE MILK COMES IN

Three or four days after the birth the colostrum you produce will start to change to mature milk. This is referred to as the 'milk coming in' and your breasts may feel uncomfortably full. Your midwife will encourage you to put your baby to the breast as often as possible, as the more he sucks the more stimulation the breasts receive to make more milk. Sucking also stimulates the production of the hormone oxytocin, which pushes the milk through

the milk ducts and into the nipples, producing a strong, tingly sensation known as the 'let-down' reflex. As the baby feeds, he also stimulates the production of prolactin which encourages the breasts to make more milk for the next feed.

Breastmilk is perfectly tailored to your baby's needs. The watery foremilk quenches his thirst, while the creamier hindmilk, which the breast produces after the first few minutes of sucking, provides nutrients and satisfies the baby's hunger. However, all babies lose weight during their first week of life. They pass meconium, a thick, black substance for the first 24 hours before starting to digest breast or formula milk. At first the meconium and urine they pass is not compensated for by the amount of food taken in. Large babies lose more weight than small ones. The average weight loss is 113 g to 198 g.

### HOW TO BREASTFEED

There are many different positions in which you can breastfeed your baby successfully. The key is to find one that is comfortable for you and easy for him to 'latch on' or

### Helping yourself

- If your breasts feel uncomfortably full, try to sit in a warm bath or shower before a feed to help the let-down reflex so your milk starts to flow before your baby latches on and starts to suck.

- Ease any throbbing by putting cold, wet flannels on your breasts.

- If your nipples become cracked or sore try to expose them to the air as much as possible to speed up healing.

- If you use breast pads in your bra to absorb extra, leaking milk, make sure you change them frequently so your nipples do not remain wet and soggy.

- The early days of breastfeeding can be difficult so try to persevere, as by six weeks breastfeeding will be fully established and your breasts will be providing the right amount of milk.

take the nipple and the surrounding dark area, called the areola, into his mouth properly. Imagine a piece of Velcro attached to your baby's bottom lip and the opposite piece attached one inch below the base of your nipple. You need to match the two together. If he is latched on properly you will see more of the areola above his top lip than his bottom one. His nose and chin will be touching your breast. When he is in the right position he can use his tongue and jaws to squeeze milk into the nipple. He should be facing you, chest to chest, and should not need to turn or twist to feed. If he is not in the right position he will end up chewing on the nipple, causing pain and possible bleeding. To remove your baby from the breast, gently insert your little finger into the corner of his mouth.

### Be comfortable

Make yourself as comfortable as you can to breastfeed and get everything you need to hand before you start, so that you are not interrupted in the middle. Many mothers breastfeed sitting on a firm chair with a cushion in the small of the back –

remember to get the cushion in place first. Others prefer to breastfeed lying down on their side with their head supported by a cushion. Choose the best position for you. A cloth or muslin square is useful to mop up any feed he brings up or 'possets'. You may find that breastfeeding makes you thirsty. This is nature's way of getting you to take more liquid, so have a glass of water within reach.

### HOW OFTEN TO FEED

Many small babies feed every couple of hours and there may be periods when your baby seems to be continuously at the breast. Generally, breastfed babies feed more frequently than bottlefed ones because they are able to digest the milk so well. As your baby gets bigger he may settle into a regular pattern but this is likely to be more frequent than the classic four-hourly feeding that the old text books used to recommend.

If your baby seems dissatisfied when feeding, you may worry that you are not producing enough milk. This is extremely rare – the World Health Organisation (WHO) estimates that only two in every 100 women are unable to produce sufficient milk to feed their babies. To ensure your baby is getting enough:

- try to have a good rest each day and eat lots of fresh foods. Cereal, fruit, a sandwich, glass of milk or beans on toast are quick, healthy snacks. Many women find their supply gets low in the late afternoon and early evening.

- ask your midwife or partner to check that your baby is taking a big mouthful of breast including the areola, as sometimes you can think you have a poor supply when your baby is not positioned properly. Listen for a glugging sound as the feed gets underway.

### BREASTFEEDING A BIGGER BABY

Babies go through growth spurts, often at six weeks and again at three months. At these times you may feel uneasy that your calm, settled, contented baby has become fractious and may seem dissatisfied. Again, the solution is to increase the frequency of feeding, to enable the extra sucking to stimulate more milk production. So long as you let your baby feed more often, he should settle back into a more reliable pattern within a few days.

### NIGHT FEEDING

At the beginning, your baby will not be able to distinguish night from day so you will need to encourage him to have his longest sleep at night. Keep night feeds low-key and he will go back to sleep more quickly:

- Don't change his nappy or turn up the lights.

- Don't be tempted to play with him or distract his attention from feeding.

- You may want to take him into bed with you to feed. This is safe, as long as you are not taking drugs or alcohol and that you make sure he does not overheat and his head is not covered by your bedcover.

- Your baby is unlikely to sleep through the night until he is at least three months old, so you must try and rest during the day to make up for the night waking.

### HOW LONG TO BREASTFEED

Breastfeeding for even a few days provides your baby with valuable antibodies to fight infection. If you continue to breastfeed for 14 weeks, studies have shown that babies can enjoy the health benefits for up to two years (see Why breast is best for your baby on pages 9–10). Some women continue for a year or more because they find it such a rewarding and enjoyable experience. It's really up to you and your circumstances.

From four months onwards your baby will start to take solid food and his dependence on breast milk as a source of nourishment will gradually decrease (see Weaning on page 28).

### GOING BACK TO WORK

It is possible to combine breastfeeding with paid employment but you need to plan ahead so your arrangement suits you, your baby, your partner, the baby's carer and your employer.

You can decide to express milk at home, which your carer can then feed to your baby in a bottle, or you may decide to switch to formula milk during the daytime and

### WHEN TO ASK FOR HELP

Ask your midwife or health visitor for help if:

- feeding is painful from beginning to end.

- your nipple bleeds.

- your breasts become hard, swollen and tender (engorged) after your milk has come in.

- your baby seems restless and dissatisfied at the breast.

- your baby takes longer than 40 minutes to feed at each breast.

- your baby feeds more than 10 times in 24 hours after he is a week old.

- your baby has fewer than three feeds in the first 24 hours or fewer than six feeds after that.

- your baby has not regained his birthweight by the time he is 10 days old.

breastfeed in the mornings and evenings only. Many mothers who return to work choose to continue the morning and evening feeds as a special time of closeness at the beginning and end of the day.

If your baby is more than six months old, you can introduce a trainer cup with a feeding spout rather than a bottle. But if you plan to switch to a bottle or organise bottlefeeds for him during the day, you need to get him accustomed to it first:

- Touch your baby's lips with the teat and encourage him to take the bottle (you can buy nipple-shaped teats, see Choosing a teat on page 24).

- Offer the milk from a small spoon. Some breastfed babies who are reluctant to switch to a bottle will happily sup from a spoon.

- Ask your partner to give your baby the bottle. Your baby will not expect a breastfeed from him.

- Offer the bottle when he is not too hungry, so he won't be frustrated by feeding in an unfamiliar way.

- Your supply of breastmilk will start to reduce once you start bottlefeeding with formula milk.

### EXPRESSING YOUR MILK

If you plan to express your own milk, you will need to get a hand or electric pump. Expressed breastmilk will keep for up to 48 hours in a fridge and up to three months in a freezer. You can buy special bags that have been made without harmful chemicals for storage.

Thaw frozen breastmilk by putting the container in a bowl of warm water. Don't use a microwave as it will heat the milk unevenly and may scald your baby's mouth.

### BREASTFEEDING AND THE ENVIRONMENT

Breastfeeding is best for the environment, as well as for your baby. For every three million babies bottlefed worldwide, 63,490,000 kg of metal is discarded in milk containers.

You may worry that today's polluted environment has affected the purity of your milk and there have been reports about dangerous chemicals, called dioxins, found in breastmilk. But the benefits of breastfeeding far outweigh the risks.

The use of organochlorines in our industries over the past 50 years has produced a certain amount of toxic waste which has entered all our bodies, so your baby would have been exposed to this as he developed in the womb whether you breast- or bottlefeed him. Recent reports suggest that these levels are now falling and, of course, formula milks may contain pollutants too.

### BREASTFEEDING AND HIV

The HIV virus can be transmitted through breastmilk. If you are HIV positive it is recommended that you do not breastfeed.

### YOUR FEELINGS

You may be overwhelmed by the powerful emotions that breastfeeding stirs in you. You may find that it cements the bond between you and your baby in a unique and fulfilling way. Many women gain a source of satisfaction from the knowledge that they are providing all the nourishment their baby needs from their own bodies. On the other hand you may feel slightly embarrassed about breastfeeding in public or aware that your partner is jealous of the intimate attention your baby is receiving and these thoughts can override any sense of contentment. Each woman's situation is different and you have to weigh up the benefits of this natural form of feeding against any possible disadvantages. If you decide that breastfeeding is not for you, or you want to stop before your baby is fully weaned, you will need to get your baby used to bottlefeeding.

Once you have made the decision to switch to bottlefeeding, you may feel guilty. However, remember that each day of breastfeeding has given your baby extra protection against infections and illnesses, by the passing on of your antibodies to him. You may also find that your energy levels are boosted once you stop breastfeeding – and if you feel positive, your baby will undoubtedly benefit, too.

# Bottlefeeding

Three-quarters of the 750,000 babies born in the UK each year are bottlefed by the time they are four months old. Your baby will be in very good company if you choose this method of feeding him. You may decide to bottlefeed straight from birth or you may want to switch over after breastfeeding your baby for a few days, weeks or months.

## YOUR BREASTS

If you bottlefeed from the start, your breasts may feel uncomfortably full for the first few days but as your baby will not be stimulating them to make milk by sucking, this feeling of fullness will soon disappear.

When changing over from breastfeeding to bottlefeeding:

- cut down gradually, replacing one breastfeed every two days with a bottlefeed, or topping up each breastfeed with a small amount of formula so your breasts start to reduce their milk supply.

- your breasts may become engorged. Relieve the discomfort by expressing by hand a small amount of breastmilk, but not too much or you will stimulate them to make even more milk.

- if your breasts feel hot, you develop a red mark on one or you start to run a temperature, you may have developed mastitis, caused by a blocked milk duct. See your GP as you will need antibiotics.

## CHOOSING A MILK

Experts agree that formula milk, usually based on cows' milk, is not, and never can be, exactly the same as breastmilk. Originally intended for calves, which have big bodies and small brains, it has had to go through many stages of processing to be made suitable for human babies, who have small bodies and big brains. Protein and salt levels have been modified and iron has been added. The main types of formula milk are:

- whey-dominant. Usually labelled as a first milk or as suitable from birth, this formula has extra whey protein added to it to bring it closer to breastmilk. Whey is watery and easier for a baby to digest than casein.

- casein-based. Slightly higher in protein than the whey formula, this milk takes longer to digest. It is sold in the UK as a 'follow-on' milk, designed to satisfy 'hungrier' babies. In fact there's no conclusive evidence to support this. The UK's Department of Health has assessed both types of milk as being suitable for babies from birth.

- rich in longchain polyunsaturated fatty acids (LCPs). Formulas including LCPs, which are known to be vital in promoting brain growth in babies, are closest to breastmilk. However, this type of milk is the most expensive option.

### THE RIGHT FORMULA

- Your baby may go through a restless period in the early evening when you think he is not satisfied. Some mothers change to a 'follow-on' milk but there is no need to as this is common behaviour for both breast and bottlefed babies. They settle down as they grow older.

- A milk which does not suit your baby may cause sickness, a skin rash or other allergic reaction. If your baby is gaining weight at around 225 g (8 oz) per week and is not showing any of these symptoms, his milk is fine. If you are not happy with the milk you are using, consult your health visitor before changing.

- Soya-based formulas are available for babies who are allergic to cows' milk

formula but you should always check with your doctor before changing as there may be other drawbacks to using soya milk, as some babies are allergic to it.

### ESSENTIAL EQUIPMENT

You will need:

- six to eight 250 ml (8 fl oz) bottles. Some types are for use with plastic throw-away liners, which collapse as the milk is sucked out, preventing your baby from swallowing too much air when he sucks. A bottle comprises a teat (see Choosing a teat on page 24); a cap to protect the sterile teat when not in use; a ring which screws on to fasten the teat to the bottle.

- two bottle brushes

- a sterilising system

- a measuring jug with a lid

- plastic knife and spoon

- Apart from breastmilk, infant formula is the only milk suitable for your baby until he is at least six months old. Goats' milk and condensed milk are not suitable foods for young babies.

- In an emergency, if you find you have run out of formula feed, you can give boiled and cooled cows' milk diluted to two-thirds milk and one-third water.

### MILK SCARES

There have been various 'baby milk scares' over recent years when traces of chemicals have been found in formula tins. Manufacturers have immediately withdrawn all suspect products from sale and extensive investigations have taken place. Health experts usually advise mothers to continue feeding their babies with their normal formula until the source and scale of the problem has been identified.

### MAKING UP FEEDS

- Follow the manufacturer's instructions on the container exactly. Never be tempted to add extra powder because your baby seems hungry. The highly concentrated milk will put a strain on his kidneys which are too immature to cope, as well as giving him a great thirst.

- Never add sugar or powdered baby food. If you think he is hungry consult your health visitor about whether you should start weaning him before he is four months old (see Weaning on page 28).

- Either pour the boiled water straight into the sterilised bottle or mix up the water and powder together in a jug first. If you do use a jug it must be sterilised before each use (see The cleaning process on page 25).

- Use the scoop provided by the manufacturer and make sure the powder is loose in the scoop. If you pack it down you will make the milk much too concentrated.

- Level off the scoop with a sterilised, plastic knife.

- Shake or stir in the powder well to dissolve it completely.

- It is usually easier to make up the day's feeds in one go. Store made-up formula in the feeding bottles with the caps on for 24 hours in a fridge.

- To reheat formula milk, stand it in a jug of hot water for several minutes. Check the temperature by shaking a few drops on to your wrist before giving it to your baby.

## HOW TO STERILISE

Bottlefeeding requires scrupulous hygiene. All sorts of bacteria thrive in warm milk so you will need to sterilise the bottles, teats and spoons you use to make up the feed thoroughly in one of three ways:

- Chemical sterilising. The steriliser you buy may be a tank or bucket shape. It must have a float to put over the bottles and teats to keep them completely submerged in a solution made up according to the manufacturer's instructions with water and sterilising liquid or tablets (available from chemists and babycare shops). The washed feeding equipment can be kept in the solution until it is needed, but it's important to check that there are no air bubbles in the

bottles, as these areas will not be sterilised. Change the solution every 24 hours and rinse the bottles and teats with cooled, boiled water to remove all traces of the solution before making up the feed.

- Steaming. An electric steam steriliser which stands on your worktop is the simplest way to sterilise. You can buy special models designed for use in a microwave.

- Boiling. This is a useful method in an emergency, such as when you have to make up an extra feed unexpectedly but it is very time-consuming. You need to boil all equipment for 15 minutes, making sure no air bubbles are trapped.

- Don't reheat milk in a microwave, as there may be hot spots that can scald your baby's mouth.

### HOW MUCH AND WHEN

- A rough guide is 65 ml of milk per pound of body weight each day but babies are individuals and their appetites will vary and your baby's appetite will soon show you how much he needs.

- Don't expect him to consume the same amount of milk as your friend's baby, even if they are the same age, and don't be surprised if he is hungrier on some days than others.

- A newborn baby will need six to eight small feeds a day. As formula milk takes longer to digest than breastmilk, bottlefed babies usually need feeding less frequently. He will probably take around 85–100 ml at each of the feeds.

- Try and feed your baby whenever he seems hungry. You will soon recognise the distinctive cry which signals that he feels empty. You are likely to settle into a routine much more quickly if he learns that his hunger will be quickly satisfied.

- Babies need to learn to give the right signals too. A newborn baby has never experienced hunger pangs before, as he was fed continuously in the womb through the umbilical cord. Be prepared for a few false alarms, as he becomes familiar with all the new sensations in his body.

- Gradually, he will reduce the number of feeds but drink more at each one, until he is taking 200 ml (7 fl oz) of milk five or six times during each 24-hour period.

- Even if you start weaning at four months, he should still be having at least four bottles of milk (200 ml/7 fl oz each) a day until he is at least five months old.

### HOW TO BOTTLEFEED

- Make sure you are in a comfortable position, with your back supported and feet flat on the floor and have everything to hand before you start.

- Support your baby's head in the crook of your arm, above the level of his stomach.

- Test the temperature of the feed with a couple of drops on the inside of your wrist. It should feel warm.

- Tilt the bottle so the teat is full to stop your baby from swallowing too much air (he will inevitably swallow some).

- Stop the feed every couple of minutes so the teat, which tends to collapse from being sucked, can resume its proper shape. You may also need to burp your

### CHOOSING A TEAT

Whichever teat you use, always ensure that there is a sufficient milk flow before feeding by turning the bottle upside down and checking that two or three drops of milk are released each second. If the milk does not flow, the teat may be blocked with a small particle of formula. If it flows faster than this, the hole may have worn. In either case, you should replace the teat. Silicone teats last up to a year; the rubber in latex ones begins to deteriorate after four weeks of use. Throw them away as soon as they stop working properly.

- The universal teat is the standard type that has been sold for many years. A cross-cut hole is better for the milk flow than a pinhole.

- An anti-colic teat lets air into the bottle as your baby sucks the milk out. This helps to ensure a steady flow of milk, by stopping the teat from collapsing. Your baby will also swallow less air, so there is less chance of him suffering from wind or colic.

- A wide-based teat has to be used with a wide-necked bottle. As your baby sucks, the teat nipple moves in and out of his mouth.

- An orthodontic or natural-shaped teat is supposed to encourage proper development of your baby's jaw and palate. The teat hole must point towards the roof of your baby's mouth, spraying the milk upwards.

baby from time to time by rubbing his back to release trapped air.

- Your baby will usually turn his head away when he has had enough. Don't force him to finish the milk.

- Throw away left-over milk, as it will no longer be sterilised, as well as any untouched bottles of milk that have been warmed up – bacteria may grow due to the warming process.

- A bottlefed baby may need additional drinks of water (see What about water? on page 26), particularly on a hot day.

### ENJOY THOSE FEEDS

Feeding your baby can be an enjoyable, intimate experience. If you are not worrying about how much milk he is getting because you can see exactly how much he takes, it should be possible to relax and make this a special time together. Cuddle your baby in your lap and enjoy looking into his eyes as he savours the experience and don't be tempted to let too many other people take over unless you want them to. One of the main advantages of bottlefeeding is that your partner can feed the baby too, helping him feel fully involved and allowing you to get some rest. Many couples take turns to feed their baby at night.

### AFTER THE FEED

Before sterilising used feeding equipment, wash it all in hot, soapy water. Clean inside the bottles with a bottle brush, taking extra care to remove any traces of milk or powder from the bottom and the neck. Turn teats inside out and hold them under running water. Check the hole is not blocked. As an extra precaution you can rub ordinary household salt around the turned-out inside to remove any traces of milk or powder.

After sterilising, drain equipment on a piece of kitchen towel. If you are using a chemical steriliser leave the bottles in it until you need them, but take the teats out after the recom-mended time, drain and store in a sterile jar.

### BANISH GUILT

You may feel guilty about choosing to bottlefeed your baby or, if you had problems breastfeeding and decided to change methods, you may experience a sense of failure.

Don't blame yourself – trying to live up to perfection is not good for you or your baby. One of the first lessons you learn as a mother is that bringing up children is not easy.

Try to remember that later on, when you are watching your teenage son playing in a football match or your daughter dancing in a school production, whether you breast- or bottlefed will seem completely irrelevant.

Once you have decided to bottlefeed, put the decision behind you and do not allow negative thoughts to spoil your relationship with your baby. Be flexible – as a mum you need to learn to overcome many hurdles and temporary setbacks.

You are a good mother if you provide love, security and encouragement for your growing baby, as well as meeting his physical needs. Don't waste precious time and energy fretting if you have to modify your plans slightly. Enjoy these months – they won't come again.

# What about water?

Not so long ago, when we were children, it was possible to drink water straight from the tap. Unaware of the risks of lead poisoning and pollution, our parents told us that water was clean, good for us and cost nothing. Today we know better. In parts of the UK, there have been pollution incidents with sewage, aluminium and other bacteria which have got into the water supply, affecting millions of consumers. Environmentalists tell us that there are leakages every day at each of the country's 400 main water treatment plants and that with chemicals, sewage, fertilizers, industrial and farmyard waste seeping into our water supply, nobody really knows what the long-term consequences may be.

On the other hand, we know that water is an essential part of a balanced diet. Babies lose more water through their kidneys and skin than adults, and spells of sickness and diarrhoea, more common in babies, can also lead to dehydration.

Breastfed babies do not need any extra water, as breastmilk has the capacity to adapt to quench your baby's thirst, even in hot weather. But if your baby is bottlefed or starting to eat solids and cutting down his breastfeeds, you will need to offer him water.

### KEEPING IT PURE

- Older houses may still have lead water pipes; ask your local water authority to check yours. Lead has been linked to nerve damage, mental impairment and anaemia in children. Slow lead poisoning does not necessarily show any symptoms.

- Run the taps for a few minutes before use to flush out any lead and reduce concentration levels.

- In some agricultural areas, nitrates have spread into the water supply from contamination by nitrogen fertilisers. Heavily farmed areas and the Southeast have been particularly badly affected. Nitrates make it more difficult for babies to absorb oxygen and have been linked to other illnesses. Boiling water can actually increase the concentration of nitrates. If there are high levels of nitrates in the water in your area, make sure your baby

eats plenty of fresh vegetables, organically grown if possible, as these are believed to counteract the effects or use bottled water.

- Pesticides are commonly found in drinking water. Filtering (see Ways with Water below) can remove some, or else use bottled water. However, bottled water is an expensive option and uses 1,000 times as much energy as tap water to produce.

- Aluminium is sometimes added to drinking water to make it clearer, even though experts have linked it to Alzheimer's disease in older people. A water filter will reduce aluminium levels.

### WAYS WITH WATER

- Tap water given to babies up to six months old must be boiled and cooled first.

- Water filters are available either in a simple jug form, which can be kept in the fridge, or one can be connected to your main water supply so all drinking water is automatically filtered. They remove chlorine, aluminium, lead, pesticides and limescale, which furs up kettles.

- Bottled still water can be given as an alternative to tap water but it should still be boiled and cooled until your baby is six months old. Check with your health visitor about which type is suitable.

- Write to your local paper and to your MP about water pollution. Join an environmentalist organisation that is campaigning against it.

- Buy a water testing kit from your local chemist or health food shop to monitor the quality of the tap water in your area.

### HELPING THE WATER SUPPLY

- You can save water by bathing your baby every other night and giving him a wash in between or by cutting down the amount of water you run.

- Use a jug for brushing his teeth rather than leaving a tap running, which wastes around 5 litres of water.

- As your child grows bigger, teach him to enjoy a shower rather than a bath and to turn off running taps when washing or cleaning teeth.

# Weaning

Between four and six months your baby will need to start eating solid foods to fuel his rapid growth, although milk will still be his major source of nourishment until he is about six months old. When weaning is under way, encourage him to develop a taste for a wide variety of foods to get him used to bulk, different flavours and textures. Only the bare essentials of feeding are covered in the following pages. For further information on feeding your child a healthy, balanced diet, *The Complete Baby and Toddler Meal Planner* (Ebury Press) by internationally acclaimed children's food expert Annabel Karmel is highly recommended.

## WHEN TO START

It's important not to hurry your baby on to solids before he is ready. If you think your baby needs to start solids before four months or he was born prematurely, your health visitor will advise you. He will still need at least four bottles of 200–225 ml until he is five to six months old (there are 65 calories in 100 ml of milk). Consider introducing solids from four months if:

- your baby shows an interest in your food.

- he starts waking again for a night feed after a period of sleeping through.

- he seems dissatisfied after a breast- or bottlefeed.

## ESSENTIAL EQUIPMENT

You will need:

- an absorbent bib with a soft fastening – leave the stiff plastic 'catch-all' types until later.

- a plastic bowl and shallow plastic spoon. Plastic won't hold the heat and shallow bowls and spoons make it easier for your baby to learn to feed himself.

- a large plastic mat or plenty of newspaper to put under your baby's seat. Weaning is a messy business!

- a blender for preparing home-cooked foods.

# Introducing solids

Choose a time of day when you can relax and your baby is not usually fractious or starving. He may be frustrated if he expects a milk feed and is presented with something completely new. So give him some of his milk feed first to take the edge off his appetite but not to fill him up completely. Seat him securely in his car seat or pushchair and offer a teaspoon of baby rice mixed with expressed breast milk, formula or cooled, boiled water. Let your baby suck the food off the spoon – don't push it into his mouth. If your baby likes it offer a second and a third spoon and then introduce it at another meal. Remember he won't be used to using a spoon so not much of it will go in his mouth. After a few days, try introducing some puréed vegetable or fruit with the rice. Be prepared for a variety of reactions – some babies spit out the food or pull faces. Others may turn their heads or even start to cry. If your baby is not interested don't force him, try again in a few days' time.

### PREPARING MEALS

- First foods must be puréed or mashed until they are completely smooth.

- Root vegetables can be boiled, steamed or baked before being puréed or mashed.

- Make sure all fruit and vegetables are fresh. If possible, use organically grown ones from a local producer.

### READY-MADE MEALS

All mothers have days when life is so busy that they open a jar, tin or packet of commercial babyfood for convenience. Don't feel guilty – it will do your baby no harm and can save you the stress of quickly trying to prepare food for a hungry, yelling

### FIRST FOODS
#### (FROM FOUR MONTHS)

*To give:*

- baby rice – a gluten-free cereal, indicated by a symbol
- puréed carrot, potato and swede
- well-mashed banana
- ready-made baby foods
- well-mashed avocado

*To avoid:*

- red meat, fish and chicken – too difficult to digest
- wheat cereals – contain gluten which can cause an allergy
- bread – contains gluten which can cause an allergy
- cows' milk – risk of allergy
- yoghurt – risk of allergy
- eggs – risk of allergy to the white
- nuts – risk of allergy
- added salt – kidneys cannot process it
- added sugar – risk of obesity and tooth decay in the future
- unpasteurised honey – risk of botulism, a form of food poisoning

baby! Check the label for the ingredients which must be listed in descending order of weight. Choose baby foods with meat, vegetables or fruit high up on that list and make sure that they contain fresh produce, free from artificial additives.

However, commercial baby foods are not ideal to give your baby on a regular basis. Reports have shown that added water and thickeners are used to bulk out the contents of jars and tins so that some products fail to meet the minimum nutritional standards doctors

## ALLERGY WATCH

You will find it easier to discover if your baby is allergic to certain foods if you introduce new tastes one by one. Allergic reactions include:

- skin rash
- red bottom
- wheeziness
- vomiting
- diarrhoea
- swollen stomach

If you have a history of eczema or allergy in your family, be particularly careful about introducing new foods. Some experts believe it is best to wait until five months before offering fruits, as young babies find it difficult to cope with the fructose (sugar) in them. Many babies

also show an intolerance to wheat products, so it is important to choose gluten-free foods. Coeliac disease is an extreme allergic reaction to gluten in wheat, rye, oats and barley. Intolerance to cow's milk, which affects about two per cent of babies under a year, can be due to a reaction to the protein in the milk or an inability to digest the lactose (sugar) also present. A severe reaction, such as swelling and difficulty in breathing, is rare (anaphylactic shock). Vomiting or a rash usually occur 12–18 hours after exposure, making it difficult to detect which food was responsible. Nuts and eggs are also common causes of allergy, because of the immaturity of a baby's digestive system.

have recommended. Meat-based baby foods may contain as little as 20 per cent meat and by adding the word 'dinner', manufacturers can cut the meat content to just 10 per cent. A banana 'flavour' pudding need not contain any banana, although a banana pudding must and some low-sugar rusks have more sugar in them than a doughnut.

Modified starch is widely used in the babyfood industry as a low-cost bulking agent. It is made from chemically treated cornflour. Some research shows that babies who eat it are unable to absorb carbohydrates properly and they may have loose stools as a result. Maltodextrin, modified cornflour, wheatstarch, starch and maize starch are other bulking agents with no nutritional value except calories.

You would not want to spend your entire life eating packet and tinned foods, so why expect your baby to do the same? Encourage him to enjoy fresh foods and he will start to take part in family meals much sooner and be ready to experiment with a wide variety of tastes.

Finally, remember that the baby food market is worth many millions of pounds to the manufacturers and magazines that carry advertising. Some editors may be under pressure to recommend commercial foods.

### DOS AND DON'TS

- If you have a freezer, cook in batches and then freeze the food in mini-portions, using an ice cube tray or purpose-made plastic baby food tray.

- Thaw and reheat food thoroughly, allowing it to cool to lukewarm before offering it to your baby.

- Wash your baby's bowl and spoon in hot, soapy water. Continue sterilising feeding bottles and teats.

- If using convenience babyfood, keep what's left in the jar in the fridge for up to 48 hours.

- Don't reheat in a microwave – it will cause hot spots in the food.

- Don't use cows' milk to mix food to the right consistency until your baby is six months' old.

### TASTY TEXTURES

From about seven months start to introduce different textures with minced or mashed foods. Again, expect him to pull a few funny faces as he gets used to the idea. It is important to move him on to these textures, however, so he can learn to chew up food. Chunky finger food will also give his hard gums plenty to chew on.

### FOLLOW-ON FOODS (FIVE TO SIX MONTHS)

Once your baby is enjoying his first foods three times a day, start to increase the amount and introduce more variety. But the consistency should still be puréed.

*Foods to try:*
- peas, sweetcorn, cabbage, broccoli, cauliflower, spinach, courgettes, turnips
- lean red meat
- chicken
- split lentils
- natural yoghurt
- apricots, peaches, stewed apples
- Cheddar cheese, cottage cheese

*Foods to avoid:*
- wheat – risk of allergy to the gluten
- eggs – risk of allergy
- nuts – risk of allergy and choking
- soft cheeses because of the risk of listeriosis, a disease which develops from food infected with the bacteria listeria
- added salt and sugar
- too many convenience foods
- unpasteurised honey – risk of botulism, a type of food poisoning
- hot, spicy foods

## EXPANDING THE MENU (SEVEN TO NINE MONTHS)

At this age, your baby's maturing digestive system will not be so sensitive to certain allergy-causing foods, such as wheat, and he may want to feed himself. You should never leave him alone to eat, especially with finger foods, as he may choke.

*Foods to try:*
- wheat-based foods like pasta, breadsticks, low-sugar rusks and toast
- cereals
- hard-boiled egg yolk
- lean red meat
- cheese, fromage frais, yoghurt

- fruits
- pulses

*Foods to avoid:*
- whole nuts – some experts believe nuts should not be given until about 18 months because of the risk of allergy, but others say that nut pastes can be used earlier than this. Check with your health visitor if you are unsure. Whole nuts should not be given until your child is five years old because of the risk of choking.
- egg white
- added salt and sugar

During the first two years of life the brain grows faster than at any other time, making essential connections between the cells that cannot be reproduced later on. Imagine a tree with large and small branches, twigs, leaves and veins on each leaf. Each part of this structure has to connect to the next part. Iron is an essential part of your baby's diet. It ensures that all these connections are properly made. By six months your baby's iron stores will be depleted so you should make sure he eats plenty of iron-rich foods to ensure his brain and central nervous system grow and develop as well as they possibly can. Foods rich in iron include red meat, green vegetables, dried apricots and egg yolk. Vitamin C helps your baby to absorb iron and can be found in potatoes, tomatoes and green vegetables.

## FAMILY EATING

From nine months, your baby can start joining in family mealtimes. He can sit in his highchair pulled close to the table and enjoy more or less the same foods as the rest of the family. He will want to feed himself and must be allowed to make a mess. Chop up his food for him then let him use his fingers or a spoon. The more independent you allow him to be, the sooner he will master the art of feeding himself with minimum mess. If you make a big issue of it he is likely to give up trying altogether. You may want to buy a bowl that sticks to the surface it is put on, as this makes it harder – but not impossible! – for your baby to tip it upside down. A large plastic bib with sleeves for him to wear while eating is also a wise investment. Your baby may be more or less fully weaned but milk should be an important part of his diet until he is at least five years old.

## VEGETARIAN BABIES

If you don't want your baby to eat meat make sure he is getting enough protein from pulses, grains and dairy products. You need to be careful about iron too – formula and follow-on milks contain extra iron but if you are still breastfeeding you may need to ask your health visitor for advice.

Vegan mothers need to ask for special advice on grain milks, soya products and ways to avoid iron deficiency.

## MILK QUOTA

Until your baby is a year old, he should have formula, follow-on formula or breastmilk as his main drink, although you can use small quantities of cows' milk in cooking from six months. From then on he can be given cows' milk instead, although he should still have 350 ml each day, including on cereals and in cooked dishes. By this age, he should be able to drink his milk from a cup, having breast or bottlefeeds as a comfort before bedtime if he doesn't want to give them up.

You can give semi-skimmed milk once your baby reaches two years old, but children under five should not drink skimmed milk because it is too low in fat, calories and other nutrients for a growing child.

### OTHER DRINKS

If you want to give extra drinks offer water. It should be boiled and cooled until your baby is six months old. Avoid fizzy mineral waters. Fruit juices and squashes contain a lot of sugar (sucrose, dextrose, maltose and fructose are all types of sugar), so always check labels. Even well diluted, they can damage your baby's growing teeth, particularly if given in a bottle or last thing at night. Squashes also contain lots of preservatives, additives and colourings, so avoid these for babies under one. An occasional drink of juice diluted with six parts water will do no harm but you may find that, once he has tasted it, he may refuse to drink water.

### GROWING UP WITH GOOD FOOD

Many toddlers prefer lots of small meals to three big ones. Unless there is a serious physical or psychological problem, most children will eat what they need to. Write down what your child actually consumes each day and you will probably find it's a lot more than you thought.

• Avoid making food a battleground by trying to force him to eat. Continue to offer a varied diet, with plenty of opportunity for him to try out new tastes. If he leaves something or seems uninterested, calmly remove the plate saying, 'Not hungry today? Never mind, we'll try again tomorrow.' There is plenty of time later on for him to establish regular eating habits.

• If you resent the amount of effort you are putting into preparing food that is left uneaten, concentrate on healthy, easy-to-prepare snacks such as vegetable and bread sticks with cheese dip or fruit chunks and fromage frais. Baked beans or a wholemeal sandwich cut into small squares are also quick, nutritious snacks.

### A SWEET PROBLEM

If you want to give sweets, choose chocolate. Eaten quickly, it has less time to attack the tooth enamel and scientists now say that, in addition to the iron it contains, chocolate may offer protection against heart disease in later life. Encourage your child to eat a sweet treat in one go, rather than continuously throughout the day, then clean his teeth.

You can always choose savoury snacks, such as low-fat corn chips, if you are out shopping and want to give your child a treat.

### KEEP IT NATURAL

As your baby grows bigger aim to give him a varied, balanced diet. If you don't rely too heavily on one particular food you won't be too worried by a new food scare. And if you prepare as much of the food yourself as you can, you are less likely to risk contamination from faulty processing, packaging or storage.

Read the labels on packaging. The longer the list, the more it has been processed. All ingredients have to be listed in order of quantity, starting with the largest amount, so if the list starts with an artificial ingredient, don't buy the product.

Natural additives can include chemicals derived from insects and wood. If you want to avoid these, too, buy a specialist book explaining what the names of such products actually mean. In the UK, each person eats around 4 kg of preservatives a year!

### PESTICIDES

- Buy local produce whenever you can. It will have a shorter journey to your dinner table and, if it's organically grown, you will be supporting a worthwhile initiative. We still don't know how harmful crop sprays may be in the long term, although some of the most lethal have now been withdrawn. But there have been no long-term studies on what happens to a person's health after a whole lifetime of exposure to pesticides, and neither do we know how the mixture of pesticides each individual experiences may affect the human body.

- Some pesticides are linked to nerve gases, strong poisons and immune system depressants. Look at the effects on Gulf War soldiers when large doses of highly toxic chemicals were sprayed on their tents and their food areas. And environmentalists believe that if farmers spray their crops too near to harvest time, this illegal action is never detected.

- Don't be put off by misshapen apples and carrots. The perfect specimens found in our supermarkets have been sprayed with chemicals to achieve that result.

- You will find that organically grown fruit and vegetables taste much better, even if they don't look so good.

- More than 100 pesticides leave residues in our food and organic farmers claim that it is no longer possible to grow pesticide-free food in the UK because the soil, water and atmosphere have all been contaminated.

- Nearly 10 years ago in the US, an environmental organisation reported that 5,500 children would eventually develop cancer from eating apples sprayed with the chemical alar.

### MEATY ADVICE

With so many recent meat scares in the UK, it is wise to resist giving hamburgers and other processed foods like sausages too often to your children. Choose lean meat instead – any chemical residues are stored in the fat, well away from an animal's vital organs. If you do cook minced beef make sure the juices run clear and the meat is not pink. Manufacturers are still reluctant to add this advice to their packaging, even though Government departments have asked them to do so.

### FOOD IRRADIATION

Irradiation bombards food with gamma rays from a radioactive source to change its chemical structure so it stays 'fresh' for a longer time. It kills bacteria in raw food (previously irradiation was used to sterilise medical equipment) and it can also make vegetables last longer.

- Some scientists believe that irradiation is not effective in killing all bugs, such as those that cause food poisoning, and that, because it destroys bad-smelling bacteria, we won't be able to detect whether the food has 'gone off'.

- Irradiation destroys vitamins naturally present in food.

- In the UK, scientists, farmers, doctors and environmentalists have objected to its use in food and the leading supermarket chains don't stock irradiated food, even though its use was approved in 1991, because there was such a strong public response against it.

- Only one UK company has a licence to irradiate food and experts believe that small quantities of herbs and spices may have been subjected to this treatment. You won't know if you are buying these, however, because manufacturers are not required to label the food if only small quantities have been irradiated.

### FOOD COVER-UP

Avoid using plastic film with plasticizers in it to cover up cheese and meat. These can migrate into the food and have been linked to cancer. Fatty foods are particularly susceptible to absorbing these harmful elements. Use greaseproof paper instead or buy clear wrap without plasticizers.

### GENETIC ENGINEERING

Food scientists have been experimenting with the bioengineering of food. This means changing its genetic structure. Chicken genes have been put into potatoes and fish genes added to tomatoes in an attempt to make them more disease-resistant or less susceptible to frost. Mad as this sounds, the Government is allowing each experiment on an individual basis. Again, current legislation means that manufacturers are not required to state that the food has been genetically engineered.

CHAPTER TWO

# Clothing Your Baby

Dressing your baby has never been easier. Gone are the cumbersome and fussy dresses, jackets and bootees that needed hand-washing and ironing. Today we have easy-care bodysuits and socks and bootees that can be thrown into the washing machine and don't need an iron anywhere near them.

The variety of styles on offer is tremendous. But don't feel you have to compete and make your child into a fashion victim. He will be perfectly happy in clothes that have been passed on from friends and family or bought at a 'good-as-new' sale. Baby clothes are usually outgrown before they are worn. You can conserve natural resources – and cut down on expenditure – by using second-hand outfits at least some of the time.

Be careful about fabrics. Some synthetic

materials make it difficult for your baby's skin to breathe. Try to stick to cottons and natural fibres whenever you can, especially for vests and other items that will lie next to your baby's skin.

### NAPPIES

Before disposable nappies were introduced in the mid-1960s, terry towelling squares with muslin liners were the only nappies available. For this reason, nappy buckets, sterilising solutions and a washing line of nappies drying in the breeze or hanging up in the kitchen were part of everyday life for new mothers, even though a washing machine may not have been. Laundering cloth nappies used to be a time-consuming and often messy process.

Disposables have revolutionised nappy-changing and the nappy bucket and washing line have been replaced by the nappy sack and pedal bin. In the UK today, more than 80% of new parents choose disposables, using a staggering eight million nappies a day.

But there are other options which include reusable nappy systems and nappy laundering services. Many parents are unaware of these, because the small companies who offer them have to compete with paper manufacturers with huge advertising budgets devoted to promoting disposables. Hospitals and health visitors as well as local councils – who are ultimately responsible for disposing of nappy waste – could all play a greater part in helping parents make an informed choice about the kind of nappies they use.

### DISPOSABLES

Disposable nappies are very convenient. They are widely available, easy to use and once they are soiled there is no messy scraping or soaking. You simply throw them away. For busy parents with many demands on their time, they are an attractive option and are generally preferred by childminders and day nurseries.

Disposable nappies are available in different sizes according to weight and are anatomically designed for girls and boys, with the bulk of the padding placed differently for each.

### WHAT'S IN A DISPOSABLE?

Most disposable nappies available in the UK contain:

- fluffed paper pulp imported mainly from Scandinavia and Canada. Manufacturing woodpulp is harmful to the environment because the ancient woodlands felled to produce the pulp are replaced by plantations which are intensively managed with pesticides and fertilisers.

- at least two different kinds of plastic produced from non-renewable crude oil resources. Some brands contain biodegradable plastic, but this requires certain conditions to biodegrade properly which are not always provided by landfill sites.

- absorbent gel. Sometimes the gel escapes and sticks to the baby's bottom. It is believed to be non-toxic but little is known about any long-term effects.

### THEIR EFFECT ON THE ENVIRONMENT

Disposable nappies are not environmentally friendly or natural:

- Huge quantities of wood pulp and plastic are used in their manufacture and, despite their name, diposable nappies are not fully biodegradable. Some parts decompose in a few years, others survive indefinitely.

- Disposable nappies account for 4% of household waste and take up a great deal of space in landfill sites. As the paper pulp decays it produces both carbon dioxide and methane, a greenhouse gas.

- You can help by lobbying nappy manufacturers to invest in more research on how to make their nappies completely biodegradable. In 1989, in reponse to pressure from environmental groups, the chlorine bleaching of paper pulp for nappies, which produces the highly toxic chemical dioxin, was abandoned in favour of more ecologically-friendly, non-chlorine bleaching methods.

### A PUBLIC HEALTH ISSUE

Disposables in landfill sites contain large amounts of untreated sewage as well as live vaccines. Following immunisation, a baby excretes the live polio vaccine for several weeks afterwards. There is a risk that these substances could contaminate groundwater supplies.

### THE COST OF DISPOSABLES

- According to British environmentalists, using disposable nappies costs roughly three times as much as using cloth nappies over a two and a half year period. This figure takes into account the cost of buying cloth nappies, as well as electricity, washing products, and wear and tear on the washing machine.

- If paper trainer pants or 'pull-ups' are used during potty training, this makes disposables an even more expensive option.

- The cost to local councils of getting rid of disposables is extra.

### CUTTING BACK

If you are uneasy about the high cost to the environment, but don't want to abandon disposables altogether, you can significantly cut back on disposables by using fabric nappies (see below) for some of the time, perhaps for the first couple of months when you are more tied to the home. Alternatively, use disposables only when you are travelling or out of the house.

### FABRIC NAPPIES

With the advantage of being both cheaper and more environmentally friendly than

disposables, fabric nappies are even more cost effective if you plan to have more than one child. Reusable nappies use fewer resources and produce less waste and pollution. If you have a washing machine, they are simple to clean once you establish a routine of soaking, rinsing and washing. According to one study, washing a baby's nappies at home may save up to five times the energy consumed by using disposables.

## PUTTING ON A NAPPY

There are a number of methods of folding fabric squares. The triple absorbent fold is most suitable for newborns, the kite and parallel folds are better for older babies. Your health visitor or midwife can also show you how.

*Triple absorbent fold*
1  Fold nappy in four, leaving top and right edges open.

## THE BARE NECESSITIES

- As cloth nappies have to be rinsed, soaked, washed and dried, you will need at least 24 to ensure that you have a daily supply of clean ones.

- Terry towelling squares – very absorbent, but bulky on newborns.

- Shaped terries are T-shaped with thicker central panel for greater absorbency and can be used instead of squares.

- Disposable one-way nappy liners to help keep skin dry and prevent nappy rash.

- Muslin squares can be used to line towelling nappies as an alternative to disposable liners. They are also handy as general-purpose nursery cloths.

- Nappy pins or plastic fasteners to secure fabric nappies.

- Elasticated or tie-on plastic pants to prevent leaks.

- Disposable nappy booster pads can be used as an option inside terry nappies for greater absorbency.

**2** Pull out top layer, creating an inverted triangle.

**3** Turn nappy over, leaving pointed edge at top right-hand side.

**4** Fold two middle layers into centre by one third.

**5** Fold by a third again, forming thick central panel.

**6** Secure with single pin.

*Kite fold*

**1** Start with unfolded nappy laid out as a diamond.

**2** Fold two sides into the middle to form kite shape.

**3** Fold top point over into centre to form triangle.

**4** Fold bottom point up towards the centre, adjusting the depth of fold to the baby's size.

**5** Secure with single pin.

*Parallel fold*

**1** Lay out nappy in diamond shape.

**2** Fold top and bottom points to centre.

**3** Fold left-hand point into middle, aligning it with top edge.

**4** Repeat with right-hand point.

**5** Secure with single pin.

### FITTED REUSABLE NAPPIES

For parents of wriggly babies who are daunted by the prospect of folding and pinning terry nappies, there are number of fitted reusable nappies on the market. These fit like disposable nappies and come either as all-in-one designs or two-part systems with washable pads and waterproof overpants. Prices vary. They tend to be more expensive than traditional fabric nappies but are quicker and easier to use.

(See Useful Addresses on pages 188–9 for more information on alternatives to disposables.)

### NAPPY WASHING SERVICES

If you are committed to using an environmentally-friendly system of nappies, a washing service provides a convenient alternative to laundering dirty nappies at home. These companies collect your dirty nappies at the same time as delivering a clean supply. They usually offer a range of reusable nappies which the customer either buys or hires. (See Useful Addresses on page 188 for information on services in your area).

### WASHING NAPPIES

To help prevent your baby developing nappy rash, it is important to wash and sterilise nappies thoroughly. With a supply of 24 nappies you should have enough to wash them every other day when you have accumulated a full load. You will need one bucket with a lid filled with sterilising solution for soiled nappies and another for wet ones. There are a number of proprietary sterilising solutions available or alternatively, and just as effectively, use:

- 5 drops tea tree oil or
- 2–3 tablespoons white distilled vinegar or
- 1 tablespoon domestic Borax

in an average-sized bucket, holding a gallon of water.

### Method

1 Prepare fresh sterilising solution every day.
2 Rinse off soiled nappies into the toilet before soaking in sterilising solution as indicated on the container. Wet nappies do not need to be rinsed first.
3 Wearing rubber gloves, wring out nappies and wash on a hot programme. Avoid biological detergents as these can irritate sensitive skin. Commercial fabric conditioners will make nappies less absorbent. Try adding half a cup of vinegar to the final rinse instead. There is no need to boil nappies, just use a 60°C wash.
4 Dry nappies. In summer the sun will dry and bleach nappies effectively. In winter dry outside on a line, on a clothes rack or in the tumble dryer. Drying nappies on radiators makes them hard and uncomfortable.

Some makes of reusable nappies have their own special care instructions. Always check the label first before washing.

### HOW TO CHANGE A NAPPY

Before you start, make sure you have:

- a changing mat or folded towel

- a clean nappy

- a plastic bag for throwing away

disposable nappy. Recycling supermarket bags is cheaper and more eco-friendly than using fragranced nappy sacks.

- warm water and cotton wool for wiping your baby's bottom

- barrier cream

1 Undo nappy and carefully wipe his bottom with the clean front portion, holding his feet safely out of the way with one hand.
2 Clean nappy area with cotton wool and water. Make sure you wipe a girl's bottom from front to back so that you avoid spreading bacteria into her vagina. There is no need to clean inside the lips of the vulva. If you are changing a boy's nappy, clean around the scrotum and penis but don't pull back his foreskin.
3 Dry nappy area well.
4 Slide a clean nappy under his bottom, apply barrier cream if used and fasten nappy.

### YOUR BABY'S STOOLS

At some point during the first 24 hours your newborn baby will pass a greenish-black, tar-like substance called meconium which filled his intestines in the womb.

### HELPING YOURSELF

- To prevent leaks, make sure that your baby's penis is pointing downwards before you fasten the nappy.

- Boys often urinate when you take off their nappy. To minimise the spray effect, place a tissue or muslin over his penis when you change him.

- If your baby is still feeding during the night, let him feed first even if he has a soiled nappy. If he is hungry he won't appreciate having to wait for his milk while you change him and he will probably soil his nappy during the feed anyway.

- Never leave your baby unattended on a changing table or bed.

When he has excreted all the meconium, your baby's stools will become a darkish yellow. Once feeding is established, he will probably soil his nappy after each feed. A breastfed baby's stools will become a mustard-yellow colour with a loose consistency. The contents of a bottlefed baby's nappy are likely to be firmer and greeny-grey. The colour and consistency of your baby's stools may vary from day to day, especially once he starts eating solids, when they will also become smellier.

### NAPPY RASH

Nappy rash is caused by bacteria in the baby's faeces breaking down urine in the nappy and releasing ammonia which irritates and burns the skin. A mild case of nappy rash may appear as small red spots on your baby's bottom. In severe cases, blisters appear and the skin becomes inflamed and sometimes infected. To prevent nappy rash:

- always change a soiled nappy at once.

- change wet nappies regularly, even super-absorbent disposable ones, as bacteria, not moisture, causes nappy rash.

- wipe and dry your baby's bottom at each change.

- ensure that fabric nappies are thoroughly washed and dried.

*Treatment*

If your baby develops nappy rash:

- use a nappy rash cream to soothe the affected area. Zinc and castor oil creams are effective, or try marigold ointment (calendula).

- avoid using soap, wipes or other products containing perfume or alcohol.

- stop using plastic pants. They prevent urine evaporating and may aggravate the condition.

- allow air to dry the skin by leaving his nappy off for at least 15 minutes after each change.

- use barrier cream such as Sudocrem or Drapolene to reduce the skin's contact with urine or try a natural treatment such as calendula (marigold) cream or chamomile and lavender. Add one drop of each essence to a bowl of warm water. Then dip the cotton wool into the solution and wipe your baby's bottom with it.

• change his nappy more frequently.

*Other causes*
• Allergy. Nappy rash can sometimes be a reaction to something that your baby has eaten and hasn't digested properly (see Allergy watch on page 31).

• Heat rash. Small blisters appear in the nappy area and on the body. Leave off plastic pants, dress your baby in lighter clothing and use fewer blankets.

• Thrush. White spots on a red rash starting around the anus and spreading to your baby's buttocks and inner thighs, caused by a yeast infection. Always consult your doctor.

• Inflamed and broken skin folds of thigh and groin due to prolonged wetness or caked talcum powder causing irritation. Make sure you dry this area thoroughly and avoid using talcum powder.

# First clothes

It is tempting to buy a lot of outfits for your baby before he is born but you will probably only need the basics as clothes are often given as gifts, or as hand-me-downs from parents with older babies. Babies grow very quickly, so it is not worth splashing out on a selection of outfits for your newborn, especially as he'll probably be sick on your favourite one as soon as you put it on him.

### CLOTHING PRIORITIES

Comfort and practicality are the most important considerations when you are choosing clothes for your baby. However smart the outfit, he will be miserable if it irritates his skin or is difficult to put on and take off.

• Clothes must be machine washable. You will have neither the time nor the energy to do a lot of handwashing.

• Look for soft, natural fabrics, such as brushed cotton or cotton fleece, which won't irritate your baby's delicate skin.

- Easy-fastening, accessible openings will allow you to change his nappy without undressing him.

- Bodysuits which fasten under the crotch help to keep the nappy in place and are warmer than ordinary vests.

- You will find it easier to dress your baby if his clothes open down the front.

### NEWBORN BASICS

- 6 bodysuits or vests
- 6 sleepsuits/all-in-one suits
- 2 knitted cardigans
- 1 hat
- 1 pair mittens
- 2 pairs bootees
- 2 pairs socks
- 1 all-in-one snow suit (for winter babies)
- 1 close-knit shawl or blanket

For the first couple of months your baby will be quite happy wearing the same clothes in the day and at night.

- Many babies hate their faces being covered, so look for items with wide, envelope-style necks.

- Check that socks, tights and bootees are big enough. If they fit too tightly they can damage the delicate bones in your baby's feet.

- Lacy knits are unsuitable for babies as small fingers can easily get caught in the holes.

### SECONDHAND CLOTHES

Baby clothes are often outgrown before they are outworn so if you are on a tight budget it is worth keeping an eye on the small ads in your local paper for secondhand clothes. Local mother and toddler groups regularly holds clothes and equipment sales (see Useful Addresses on page 188).

### FABRICS

*Natural fibres*

Comfortable and hard-wearing, natural fibres are made from renewable resources and are recyclable, so they have less impact on the environment.

- Cotton is widely used in baby clothes. Unlike wool, it rarely irritates sensitive skin. Choose garments made from 100% cotton wherever possible. It is often blended with synthetics like polyester, so check the label carefully.

- Clothes made of cotton jersey, brushed cotton, cotton corduroy and cotton fleece are both soft and warm. Pure cotton underwear allows sweat to evaporate and will help to prevent your baby overheating.

- Wool is a popular choice for baby knitwear, but it can often irritate the skin and is best worn as an outer layer only.

- The delicate nature of other natural fibres such as linen and silk means that they are unsuitable for baby clothes.

### Synthetic fibres

Largely produced from oil, a non-renewable resource, synthetics are often cheaper and easier to care for than natural fibres. But they are not a good choice for baby clothes as they don't allow sweat to escape and dry as efficiently. Sweat can lead to irritation between the folds of skin and increase the risk of overheating. Synthetic fibres include:

- polyester

- acrylic

- polyamide.

Synthetic blends such as polyester and cotton are more comfortable to wear.

### Fabric finishes

Fabrics, particularly cottons and poly-cottons, are often treated with finishes to make them crease-resistant or fire-retardant or to prevent shrinkage. The most commonly used finishes are resins, such as formaldehyde polymers, which can irritate sensitive skins. New baby clothes should always be washed before wearing to minimise any risk of irritation or allergic reaction from these chemicals. Other finishes include starches which are used to stiffen fabrics such as denim and some types of cotton. These usually wash out well.

### DRESSING YOUR NEWBORN

Getting clothes on and off a small baby can be a struggle. Many babies hate being naked and the task is made even more difficult by their flailing limbs and disproportionately large, floppy heads. Your baby may cry when you change his clothes, try to keep calm yourself and handle him gently but firmly. If your movements are clumsy or tentative he will only become more agitated and the process will take longer. Don't change him unless you really have to, sponge off any possets instead. To minimise fuss:

- always take his clothes off in a warm room. Babies lose body heat very quickly and he will be more miserable if he is chilly or in a draught.

- when putting his vest on, roll it up and stretch the neck hole as wide possible so you don't have to tug it over his head.

- roll up the sleeves and stretch the cuffs before feeding his arms through.

- talk to him reassuringly while you dress and undress him, so he can concentrate on your voice.

### OVERHEATING

It is important that babies are kept warm, but it is also essential to guard against overheating, which can be a factor in cot death.

If he is warmly dressed because he has been outside, take off your baby's outdoor clothes when you bring him into the house even if he has fallen asleep in his pram. Sleeping in direct sunlight or next to a hot radiator will also cause overheating. If he is in his bouncy cradle indoors with a room temperature of 20°C, your baby should be warm enough in three layers of clothing: a vest, all-in-one suit and a light blanket or cardigan.

## CLOTHING FOR OLDER BABIES

As your baby grows, the clothes he wears will be subjected to rougher treatment and will have to be harder-wearing than his first garments. He will also need a more varied wardrobe. For example, when you are trying to establish a bedtime routine you may find it helpful to change him into nightclothes. When he starts solids, his clothes won't escape the mess however large the bib, so it's important that they are well made enough to withstand repeated washing. And when your baby begins crawling he will need clothes that allow him to move freely and which protect his arms and legs. It makes sense to buy clothes on the large side so that there is some room for growth, but check that they are not so big and baggy that they interfere with crawling or his first unsteady steps.

## IN THE WASH

From the day that you bring your baby home it will seem as though the washing-machine is constantly on the go. Nappies which leak before you have the chance to change them and milk that's brought up on a regular basis ensure that the laundry basket is always full.

You may not have given your washing powder or liquid much thought until now, but certain formulas are unsuitable for baby clothes because some of the chemical ingredients can irritate sensitive skin. These are:

- enzymes

- chlorine bleaches

- perfumes

- optical brighteners (chemicals which make white fabrics appear whiter)

Used in biological and enzyme formulas, they are also found in combined detergents and conditioners. To minimise the risk of washing agents irritating your baby's skin, use non-biological formulas, pure soap flakes or products designed for people with sensitive skin. If you handwash clothes, rinse them thoroughly as detergent residues can also cause irritation. Running washed clothes through an extra rinse cycle can help prevent this.

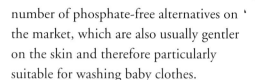

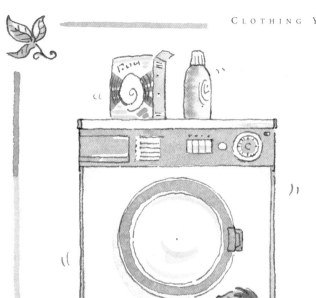

number of phosphate-free alternatives on the market, which are also usually gentler on the skin and therefore particularly suitable for washing baby clothes.

- Run your washing machine only when you have a full load to help cut your electricity bills, save water and minimise phosphate pollution.

- Wash lightly soiled clothes on a short programme rather than a long, water-and-energy-wasting hot wash.

- Tumble-drying, although convenient, consumes a lot of electricity. Air drying your baby's clothes when you can will save energy, too.

*Dry-cleaning*

Clothes which can only be dry-cleaned are not suitable for babies. Not only are they impractical – dry-cleaning is expensive and babies are not fussy about where they bring up milk – the process involves harsh solvents, which give off powerful fumes and are highly toxic.

The most commonly used dry-cleaning solvent is perchloroethylene (represented by

HELPING THE ENVIRONMENT

- Phosphates in cleaning agents, such as washing powder and liquids, upset the ecological balance of the environment. In rivers and lakes where phosphate levels are high, the algae which feed on them become so prolific that fish and other aquatic life cannot survive. There are a the letter P in a circle on cleaning labels) which has been identified as a probable carcinogen. It is an organochlorine, a group of chemical compounds which deplete the ozone layer and whose manufacture and disposal causes toxic waste.

### FIRST SHOES

Socks and bootees are all that your baby needs until he starts walking. Because the bones in his feet are malleable and easily damaged, anything which covers his feet (from socks to bedcloths) must allow plenty of room for movement.

Once your child is steady on his feet and walking outdoors he will need a proper pair of shoes. When you buy him his first pair, take him to a shoe shop where the staff are trained to fit children's shoes. The assistant will check that he is able to walk without curling his toes and then measure the length and width of his feet. When your child tries on a pair, encourage him to walk around the shop so the fit can be checked properly. The assistant should also check the shoes when he is standing still to ensure that his feet are not restricted in any way.

### FOOTWEAR PRIORITIES

When buying a pair of shoes for your toddler, look for:

- a sturdy and hard-wearing design. Leather is the most durable material and allows the skin to breathe so that feet do not get too sweaty.

- fastenings should be adjustable and hold the shoe securely on to the foot. Avoid laces as they tend to come undone – buckles and velcro are easier to fasten.

- non-slip, flexible soles.

### GOOD FOOTCARE

- Encourage your child to go barefoot on safe, non-slippery surfaces. It strengthens the muscles needed for walking.

- Keep toenails short, cutting straight across the top of the nail to prevent ingrowing toenails.

- Shoes mould to the wearer's feet, so never use secondhand shoes.

# CHAPTER THREE

# Bathing and Bedtime

A regular routine which starts with a bath or wash and ends with a goodnight kiss will help your baby learn what to expect at the end of the day and encourage him to settle in the evenings, improving both your chances of a good night's sleep!

## Bathtime

Bathtime can be an enjoyable experience for both of you. It may be scary to begin with, holding a slippery, wriggly newborn with one hand but, as he grows older, he's likely to revel in the feel of warm water and will splash and play happily, while you gently sponge away the day's dirt and grime.

### NEWBORN SKIN

Newborn skin is very thin and delicate. In the womb a baby's skin is protected by a creamy substance called vernix which prevents it from becoming waterlogged with the amniotic fluid surrounding him. At birth there may be some vernix left on your baby's skin. Don't clean it away as it will continue to protect and moisturise the skin before being reabsorbed.

When your baby is a couple of weeks old, he may develop milk spots. These

### TOPPING AND TAILING

Very young babies don't need to be bathed every day, two or three times a week is fine. Some newborns hate being undressed and immersed in water. If your baby is upset by bathing you can wash him just as well by 'topping and tailing'.

For this you will need:

- a bowl of warm water

- a small dish of cooled, boiled water for his eyes

- a soft towel, preferably with a hood

- cotton wool

- a nappy and a change of clothes.

Babies lose heat very quickly so, before you start, make sure that the room is warm and that there are no draughts.

- Undress your baby, leaving his nappy on, and wrap him in the towel.

- Clean his face with damp cotton wool, then with a fresh piece, moistened with cooled, boiled water, clean one eye, starting at the top of the nose and wiping outwards to avoid spreading any infection such as 'sticky eye' or conjunctivitis. Do the same for the other eye with a new piece of moistened cotton wool.

- Wipe your baby's head, hands and feet, leaving his nappy area until last, making sure to clean in all the creases at the top of the thigh.

- Finish off by dressing your baby in a clean nappy and a change of clothes.

white spots are just a sign that the skin is settling down. They will disappear without any treatment.

During the first weeks of life your baby's skin will continue to thicken and harden. It may also become dry and flaky but it's not necessary to treat it with special baby bath and moisturising creams. Recent research suggests that these products have little effect and that it is better not to interfere with the skin's natural hardening processes.

### BATHING YOUNG BABIES

For the first few months your baby will be too small for a normal-sized bath, so you will need a baby bath with a non-slip surface where he will be safe and feel secure. Place the bath on a surface at hip height or on a special stand if possible to protect yourself from back strain.

You can bath him in the basin but you must check that both taps are turned firmly off before you put him in. You may also need to tie a cloth round the hot tap, so that it will not burn your baby if he accidentally touches it.

### SAFETY FIRST

Bear in mind that even a few centimetres of water can be dangerous. Follow these guidelines to keep your baby safe:

- Check that the room is warm enough, around 24°C is ideal.

- Keep the bath shallow, 5–8 cm of water is plenty.

- Bathwater should be no hotter than 29.4°C. Always add cold water first and top up with hot. A floating bath thermometer is helpful until you get used to the feel of the water, then you will be able to test it with your elbow or the inside of your wrist (not your hand, which is less sensitive).

- Make sure that you have everything ready before you start.

- NEVER leave your baby unattended, even for a few seconds to answer the phone. Wrap him up and take him with you. Children under the age of five should be supervised at all times in the bath.

### INTO THE WATER

- When the bath is ready, undress your baby and clean his nappy area before wrapping him in a towel.

- Wipe his face and ears with damp cotton wool. It is easier to wash his head before he goes in the bath, so tuck his body under your arm (the 'football carry'), supporting his head with your hand, lean over the bath, rinse his hair and pat it dry (see Hair care on page 62).

- Once he is in the bath, make sure that his head and shoulders are supported at all times. Hold him gently but firmly at the top of his arm furthest away from you so that his shoulders are supported by your forearm across his back: if he feels insecure or slips under the water even for just a second he will frighten himself and it may put him off bathing for some time.

- Use as few bath toiletries as possible on your baby's skin (see Baby toiletries on pages 63–8). Soap has a very drying effect as well as being hard

to hang on to. Bath preparations that you add to the water are less harsh, especially hypoallergenic ones, and are easier to manage.

### BATHING OLDER BABIES

Between three and six months your baby will outgrow his bath and be ready to move into a normal bath. But the steep sides can appear daunting from a baby's perspective. To help him get used to it, try putting him in his bath inside the big one before making the transition. There are a variety of baby bath seats available, from shaped foam pads to specially designed plastic models, but these are an unnecessary expense.

When your baby is able to sit up

unsupported, he will take a much more active part in bathtime. Not only will he enjoy splashing around, he will also start to amuse himself with toys. Plastic ducks, boats, watermills and other more sophisticated bath toys are great fun, but a sponge, a mug or a clean, empty shampoo bottle minus the lid and mug can be just as entertaining. If he has an older sibling, sharing a bath will save time and water.

## BATHROOM HAZARDS

Now that your baby is much more curious about his environment, you will have to be even more vigilant about safety in the bathroom:

- Although he is older, don't use more than 10–13 cm of water in the bath. Never leave your baby unattended in the bath, nor with an older sibling, especially if he is under five. A child can drown in less than 8cm of water. If you have to leave the room, take them with you.

- Use a non-slip mat in the bath.

- Check the water temperature before you put him in. Set your water heater to less than 54°C so that even if the hot tap is run accidentally, it won't result in a serious scald.

- Turn taps off tightly, cover them with a flannel or special tap sleeve to prevent scalding.

- Make sure that adult toiletries, perfumes, cosmetics and medicines are safely out of reach. These products are responsible for many of the poisonings that take place in the home.

- Discourage boisterous play. Standing up unsupported and jumping could result in a fall.

- Avoid letting the water out of the bath while your baby is still in it. The noise and the sensation of the water gurgling and draining away may frighten him.

Why not get in and join him yourself from time to time?

### BATHING A TODDLER

Boisterous toddlers need close supervision at bathtime to prevent them slipping or trying to climb out of the bath. Turning on taps, emptying out bottles of shampoo and baby bath are also favourite pastimes, so be on your guard and never leave your child unattended.

At this age, he may insist on doing things by himself. At bathtime you can encourage this independent streak by showing him how to wash himself with his own special sponge or flannel.

### CLEANING TEETH

As soon as your baby cuts his first teeth at around six months old, make cleaning his teeth part of the daily routine. Looking after your child's milk teeth is an investment for the future: serious decay in first teeth can affect the development of second teeth. At first you will simply be getting him used to the idea, so it's not important how long you spend doing it.

- Use a miniscule amount of baby toothpaste on a soft, small-headed baby toothbrush, clean finger or piece of muslin.

- Rub teeth gently.

- Clean the gums even where there are no teeth as this will get rid of bacteria, providing a healthy environment when the teeth come through.

- Rinse the brush in cooled, boiled water if your baby is under six months old and gently clean around the inside of his mouth.

## HAIR CARE

Until your baby is about 12 weeks old you can simply rinse his hair with clean water or use water with a little bath lotion dissolved in it.

To wash a young baby's hair:

• wrap him a towel.

• using the 'football carry' (see Into the water on page 59), hold him close to the bath or sink and gently wet his head with your hand.

• if you are using bath lotion, dip a flannel in clean water and rinse off any lather.

• dry your baby's head carefully with a soft towel.

To wash an older baby's hair use a mild, non-sting shampoo once or twice a week. In between his hair can be rinsed with clean water. Only use one application of shampoo, making sure that you rinse his hair thoroughly. Take care not to get shampoo or water in his eyes. Not all babies enjoy having their hair washed. You can make the process less stressful for your child by:

• keeping hair-washing to a minimum. Avoid doing it when he has his bath so that it doesn't spoil his fun.

• rinsing his hair with a wet flannel rather than pouring water over his head which may frighten him.

• using a hair shield which fits around the hairline like a halo to prevent water and shampoo running down on to his face.

• letting him pour water on his head himself as part of a game.

If none of these measures help, stop. Leave it for a week or so and try again. Meanwhile, keep his hair reasonably clean with just a sponge and a damp brush.

- He will probably try and grab the toothbrush while you're doing it, so give him one of his own.

- Try and clean his teeth twice a day, once after breakfast and once before bed, as part of his routine.

- With reluctant toddlers, make a game out of teeth cleaning by pretending the toothbrush is a train, or similar.

- When your child is old enough to brush his own teeth, you will need to check his handiwork and finish them off for him.

# Baby toiletries

In any supermarket or pharmacy there is a bewildering range of baby toiletries from soaps, shampoos and bath lotions to talcs, moisturisers and barrier creams. Not all of these are essential or necessarily desirable. The safest and cheapest method of keeping a young baby clean is to use plain water with mild soap or baby lotion on dirty areas.

### THE CASE AGAINST TOILETRIES

- Products which are highly perfumed, produce lots of bubbles or contain known allergens, such as lanolin, may cause a skin reaction. If your baby's skin is easily irritated, it's important to test any new bath or skincare products. Dab a little on a small area of skin on his forearm or behind his ear and leave for 24 to 48 hours. If the area goes red or swells up, do not use the product.

- Natural odours provide a newborn baby with important information about his environment. He recognises his mother by smell, which also helps him to target the breast when he is hungry. Strong synthetic fragrances are undesirable because they interfere with these subtle messages.

- Over-exposure to chemicals can affect the development of your baby's immune system. Keeping toiletries to a minimum is a constructive way of limiting his exposure to potentially harmful substances.

## WHAT'S ON OFFER

*Soaps*

Soap is a strong de-fatting agent, which means it takes the natural oils and fats out of the skin. It has an acid/alkali (PH) balance of nine, whereas human skin has a PH balance of between five and six. It's best to avoid using it altogether during the first six weeks of your baby's life when his skin is at its most delicate. Even when he is older soap should be used sparingly. Mild baby soap or hypoallergenic varieties are less likely to dry or irritate his skin.

*Bath lotions*

- An alternative to soap. Most lotions are perfumed and produce bubbles when a capful is poured into the bath. They can also be used to wash your baby's hair.

- For babies with very dry skin or eczema, there are lotions available which will help to moisturise and soothe the skin. Some are lanolin-based, others use mineral oil or soya oil. They are more expensive, but if your baby suffers from a chronic skin problem your doctor may

be able to give you a prescription (see Eczema, pages 123-6).

If you use oil-based bath lotions regularly:
- they can break down the surface of the water, allowing it to enter the vagina and cause bladder infections.

- they can make the bath very slippery.

- some leave a greasy residue, so the bath and any bath toys will need to be cleaned regularly.

- rubber bath mats will perish more quickly.

*Baby oils*

Usually mineral-oil based, derived from petro-chemicals, these preparations can be added to the bath to moisturise very dry skin, but they can block pores. Natural oils such as sweet almond oil and ordinary olive oil make effective moisturisers (see Cradle cap on page 123).

*Shampoos*

Choose a mild, non-sting shampoo or an all-in-one shampoo and conditioner specially formulated for babies.

### Moisturisers

Many babies develop dry skin as they grow older. Ordinary soap, hot water and highly fragranced or coloured toiletries have a drying effect, so where possible choose hypoallergenic and fragrance-free products. There are many specially formulated baby skin creams on the market to soothe and moisturise dry skin.

However, less expensive and equally effective alternatives are available from the chemist:

- aqueous cream is both soothing and moisturising. It is cheaper than other alternatives and is available on prescription if your baby has a skin problem. It can also be used as a substitute for soap although it does not lather.

- E45 cream, which contains hypoallergenic lanolin

- paraffin-based creams such as Diprobase.

- essential oils such as sweet almond oil.

### Talcum powders

Although your own mother probably remembers sprinkling you with baby powder after a bath, it's not necessary and it can make your baby's skin very dry. If you do use talcum powder, make sure you apply it from your hand rather than shaking it directly on to your baby to prevent him inhaling the very fine dust. Check that the powder does not cake in the deep creases at the top of his thighs where it will irritate his skin.

### Baby lotions

Applied with cotton wool, baby lotion can be used to clean the nappy area. However, on a very young baby it is better to use pure water.

### Barrier creams

The acid in your baby's urine and faeces can irritate his skin, causing nappy rash (see Nappy rash on page 48). Preparations such as zinc and castor oil cream form a barrier which helps protect your baby's skin, especially at night when he's in the same nappy for a long time.

*Baby wipes*

Although convenient for cleaning the nappy area, baby wipes contain strong ingredients, including preservative, alcohol and fragrance and they are expensive. Some brands are suitable for wiping hands and faces as well. If you feel that wipes are necessary, look for makes that are free of chemicals as these are gentler on the skin.

However:

- using ordinary water and cotton wool is just as effective for cleaning your baby's bottom.

- a damp cloth stored in a plastic bag can be used to wipe his hands and face when you're out.

## NATURE CARE

Herbal remedies and essential oils have been used for thousands of years in bathing and skincare preparations. A number of companies produce high quality natural cosmetics, including babycare products. Many operate environmentally friendly manufacturing and retailing policies, by avoiding unnecessary packaging and using refillable, recyclable containers.

- Many of these products contain plant extracts with natural cleansing or healing properties. Plants with moisturising or soothing properties include aloe vera, marigold (calendula), chamomile and jojoba.

- They are easily absorbed by the skin. Products containing petro-chemically derived substances such as mineral oil can block the skin's pores.

- They contain fewer detergents, preservatives and emulsifiers so are less likely to irritate sensitive skin.

- Add 2–3 drops of Bach Rescue Remedy or a chamomile tea bag in your baby's bathwater to help relieve dry skin.

## ANIMAL TESTING

It is not always easy to establish which products are cruelty-free because some manufacturers do not label their products clearly or make confusing statements. 'This product has not been tested on animals' can mean that the finished product has not been tested on animals but the ingredients may have been. A growing number of companies now test their products by using, for example, cell cultures in test tubes, human volunteer studies and other non-animal based techniques.

Companies which do not test their products on animals have been put on an approved list by animal welfare groups (see Useful Addresses on pages 188–9). To qualify for inclusion manufacturers must not undertake or commission any animal tests now or in the future and neither the finished product or its ingredients should have been tested on animals in the past five years.

Many of the ingredients in cosmetics and toiletries are derived from animals. These include collagen, stearic acid, gelatine and tallow.

## PRODUCT LABELLING

If your baby has sensitive skin or you are concerned about his exposure to chemicals which may cause an allergic reaction, choose products which list their ingredients. By the end of 1998, British manufacturers will be obliged by law to provide a complete list of ingredients on the product label in descending order of quantity. Many

## READING THE LABEL

Common terms used in product labelling include:

- hypoallergenic – excludes substances most likely to cause an allergic reaction.

- fragrance-free – may contain a single fragrance, often to mask the smell of other ingredients.

- unperfumed – contains no perfume at all.

- PH-balanced – a PH value close to that of human skin (around PH5.5).

manufacturers already do this. The most common ingredients in toiletries are:

- water (often listed as aqua).

- fragrance. If your baby's skin reacts to a product the most likely cause is perfume. Try a hypoallergenic or fragrance-free alternative.

- colour.

- surfactants. These are chemical compounds used to make products dissolve in water and foam. Without surfactants shampoo would not lather, bath lotion would not dissolve and bubble bath would not bubble.

- preservatives. These inhibit the growth of bacteria and mould to make sure that a product does not deteriorate during its shelf life. Preservatives are required by law if the product has a shelf life of less than 30 months. They are also a common cause of allergy.

# Bedtime

The amount of sleep your baby needs and his sleeping patterns are unique to him. Some babies settle quickly into regular routines, sleeping through the night after only a few weeks, others resist napping during the day and rarely have an unbroken night until they are school age. If you have a wakeful baby you may worry that he isn't getting enough sleep but as long as he is happy and healthy you can be sure that he is, although you won't be.

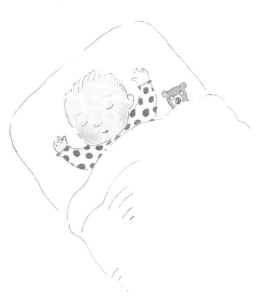

## NEWBORN SLEEPING PATTERNS

For the first six weeks or so your baby may sleep up to 18 hours a day. Newborn babies are unable to distinguish day from night so that, instead of being active by day and sleeping at night, he will sleep and wake right around the clock.

During this time, sleeping and feeding are very closely connected (see Breastfeeding on pages 8–18). The amount he sleeps will be determined by how big he is and how often he needs to feed. As a rule, the lower his birthweight, the more often he needs to feed. Premature babies tend to sleep more than those born full term and you may even have to wake him every three hours or so to feed him. How you choose to feed your baby may also affect his sleep patterns. As breastmilk is more easily digested than formula, a breastfed baby may wake more frequently to feed than one who is bottlefed.

## WHAT WILL WAKE HIM?

Your newborn baby will probably fall asleep immediately after feeding. He will sleep quite deeply and be oblivious to most external stimuli. Because his respiratory system won't have matured fully, he may grunt, snuffle or even sneeze when he is asleep. These noises are perfectly normal and he will soon grow out of them. When he wakes it will probably be due to:

- hunger
- he is too hot or too cold
- a dirty nappy
- wind

Once his physical needs have been met and with a little cuddling and comforting, your newborn will fall asleep again quite quickly. If he has trouble settling, swaddling may help.

### SWADDLING

Some newborns sleep better when they are swaddled, possibly because it mimics the constraining sensations of being in the womb. Wrapping your baby gently but firmly in a shawl, thin blanket or flannelette sheet will make him feel secure, keep him warm and provide reassuring physical contact with something soft. A baby will often jerk and twitch before falling asleep. Swaddling prevents these involuntary

movements keeping him awake.

To swaddle your baby, follow the illustration above or ask your midwife to show you how.

## HEALTHY SLEEPING

Research shows that overheating can be a contributory factor in cot death. To prevent your baby from becoming too hot:

- place him on his back to sleep.

- keep his room at a steady temperature, 18°C is ideal.

- avoid using too many covers. A sheet and two or three blankets is sufficient for a room temperature of 18°C.

- duvets and pillows should not be given to babies under 12 months.

- use the 'Feet to Foot' method of making up the cot so that your baby's head is always uncovered. Position your baby so that his feet are at the foot of the cot, turn the top sheet down over the top edge of the blankets away from his head and tuck in around the mattress edges so that he can't wriggle down underneath the bedding.

- make sure that cot bumpers are fastened securely and that you leave a gap of at least 15 cm between the mattress and the bottom of the bumper so that air can circulate.

## WHOSE BEDROOM?

While your baby is needing night feeds, it is often easier to have him in your room close to the bed so that when he wakes or needs feeding you can attend to him with the minimum of disturbance. A drop-sided cot which can be adjusted so that your baby's mattress is level with your bed may be useful as it allows him to sleep next to you without actually sharing your bed (see also Your baby's bed, page 144).

Some parents find that they don't sleep soundly with the baby in their room, as they are woken by every whimper and snuffle. In these circumstances it is probably more relaxing if your baby sleeps in a separate room.

## SHARING YOUR BED

If you are breastfeeding you may prefer to bring him into bed with you and feed him lying down in case either of you falls asleep. Sharing a bed with your baby is quite safe, in many cultures babies always sleep with their parents. A common fear is that you may inadvertently crush or smother your child when you turn over in the night. There is no risk of this happening in normal circumstances, you will instinctively compensate for this tiny extra body when you move in your sleep.

However, recent research suggests that bed-sharing should be avoided if either parent has:

- drunk alcohol prior to sleeping
- taken illegal drugs or sleeping pills
- is a smoker

For most parents it is easier to settle for one approach rather than the other. Letting your baby sleep with you sometimes and at others insisting that he sleep in his own bed will confuse him and disrupt any sleep routines that you may be trying to establish.

*The advantages:*
- greater intimacy with your baby
- convenient for feeding
- baby may wake less
- more likely to settle quickly

*The disadvantages:*
- a difficult habit to break
- as your baby grows the less comfortable it is for you
- it limits your privacy
- being with your child day and night might leave you feeling that you have no physical or emotional space to yourself.

## A BEDTIME ROUTINE

Lack of sleep and broken nights are facts of life for the parents of a young baby. It is unlikely that your baby will drop his night feeds before his weight reaches 5 kg (usually between three and five months) as he needs to feed frequently to sustain his rapid growth rate.

Although there is little you can do to make your baby drop his night feed – he'll enjoy the comfort aspect of it, too – once he does start to sleep through the night, a bedtime routine will help your baby fall asleep and settle again if he wakes up later in the night.

To establish good sleeping habits you must first help your newborn baby differentiate between night and day by:

- stimulating him while he is awake during the day

- putting him in a different room to his bedroom for his daytime naps

- darkening his room at bedtime by drawing the curtains, for example.

- keeping the night feeds as quiet and peaceful as possible – resist the temptation to play with him.

- Introduce a bedtime routine during his first few weeks of life. He will eventually learn that that sequence of events signals

## HELPING YOUR BABY TO SETTLE HIMSELF

As he grows older it's important to follow the same bedtime routine each night if you want him to fall asleep by himself:

- Don't overstimulate him with loud or boisterous play in the hour or so before bed.

- Decide on a realistic bedtime. If you want him in bed by 6.30 pm and he only starts to feel sleepy at around 8 pm you will have difficulty.

- Give him his last breast- or bottlefeed, but don't allow him to fall asleep.

- Settle him in his cot with his favourite toys and comfort object if he has one.

- Say goodnight to him and leave the room without waiting to see if he settles.

- Avoid patting, rocking or singing him to sleep, you will be putting him to sleep rather than letting him fall asleep on his own.

- Leave the door slightly ajar so that he can hear what is going on in the rest of the house. Loud music or noisy conversation may keep him awake, but a low level of background or white noise is reassuring for him.

- If he cries, wait five minutes before going back to him. Many tired babies cry for a few minutes before they sleep.

bedtime, helping him to make the transition from waking to sleeping. At first this routine will be very simple: bathing or washing your baby, changing him into his nightclothes, feeding him and putting him down in his cot in his dark bedroom. As he grows you can develop his routine by including looking at a book together before saying goodnight to the rest of the family.

### DAYTIME NAPS

Most babies have their wakeful times during the day. For some this may be the middle of the morning, for others it is late afternoon. Now that he is taking notice of his surroundings, it is important to provide him with stimulation: play with him and talk to him, enjoy plenty of physical contact with him and offer him a change of scene by taking him out for a walk with you in the pram or in the baby sling. He will also enjoy watching you carry out your chores if you put him in a baby seat or prop him up in his pram and move him around the house with you.

As he grows these wakeful periods will get longer and, if you are fortunate, by the time he is three or four months old he may have settled into a daytime routine of mid morning and early afternoon naps.

# Sleep problems

Up to six months, the sleep problem is yours, not his, as your baby will sleep for as long as his body tells him to. This may not be long enough for you, but he has no control over his body functions and he will only be kept awake by hunger, discomfort or illness. After around six weeks he will become more wakeful and alert but his sleeping and feeding habits will still be closely linked so that he will probably fall asleep after being fed and wake before his next feed.

Babies can start having sleep problems at around nine months. By now your child is aware of his surroundings and is able to keep himself awake. Although he may be sleepy during his last feed he probably won't fall asleep at the breast or on the bottle.

### WHY WON'T HE SETTLE?

• He doesn't want to miss out on the activity around him.

## A SLEEP PROGRAMME

Coping with a baby who fights sleep at bedtime or regularly wakes in the night and won't settle is exhausting and stressful for you and your child and affects family life. Once your baby is six months old you can try to settle him by following a sleep programme. One such programme is *The Baby and Toddler Sleep Programme* by Dr John Pearce (published by Vermilion, priced at £7.99). Sleep programmes are a tried and tested method of dealing with these problems but both you and your partner have to be committed to introducing one. Many parents have been successful in just a few days.

- Dedicate a week to introduce a sleep programme, preferably when you have no other commitments.

- On the first night, settle your child in his cot and leave the room. If he cries, go back after a couple of minutes and settle him by patting or stroking him, but don't pick him up.

- Leave the room and, if he cries, leave him for a few minutes longer before returning and calming him.

- Repeat the procedure as many times as it takes for him to fall asleep, leaving a slightly longer interval each time.

- On subsequent nights, follow the same routine. Consistency is crucial. If you relent and pick him up you will have to start all over again.

You may find it distressing to leave your child to cry even for a short period, but a sleep programme is usually very effective, so it's worth persevering. It may take about ten days before your baby learns to fall asleep by himself. Expect occasional relapses: changes to his routine, teething or illness will probably disrupt his sleep patterns. If this happens, reintroducing the sleep programme will usually sort things out.

- He doesn't want to be separated from you.

- He is overtired – he may be physically exhausted but is too anxious and tense to relax enough to fall asleep.

- He is unwell.

With a fretful baby who won't settle at bedtime, the temptation is to put him to sleep by holding him, rocking him or walking around with him until he falls asleep in your arms. Although this may work in the end, your baby will learn to rely on you to put him to sleep and when he wakes in the night he will need you to settle him again so it's important he learns to go to sleep on his own (see Helping your baby to settle himself, page 73).

### NIGHT WAKING

If your baby wakes in the night he may simply be uncomfortable:

- Check that he's neither too hot nor too cold. Feel the back of his neck rather than his hands which may be cool if they are outside the blanket.

- Check whether his nappy needs changing.

- If he has stopped night feeds, don't offer him milk to send him back to sleep, as he may start to associate night waking with feeding.

Even if he seems wide awake, avoid playing with him, speak to him softly, pat his back or stroke his head until he is calm and then quietly leave the room.

Health problems such as ear or chest infections may prevent your baby from sleeping. If your settled baby suddenly starts to sleep badly or if he has been unwell and his sleep patterns don't return to normal after a few days, a visit to the doctor will establish whether the problem has a physiological cause.

### FINALLY SETTLED

When your baby has established a proper sleep pattern, try to disrupt it as little as possible:

- Avoid altering naptimes or bedtime to compensate for lost sleep. A later bedtime is no guarantee that your baby will sleep later in the morning. He may simply wake up tired and fractious at the usual time.

- A catnap late in the afternoon may keep him going well beyond his normal bedtime.

- Don't drop his afternoon nap too soon. He will get overtired and overwrought and this can make it diffcult to get him to sleep in the evening.

### SLEEP CLINICS

If your child is well and still has problems sleeping, your doctor or health visitor may suggest going to your local sleep clinic. Run by health visitors, it provides parents with information and advice on sleep problems. Many take a holistic approach, taking into account the needs of the parents and the baby. At your first visit you will probably have an assessment interview to try and establish the cause of the problem. You may be asked to keep a sleep diary to help draw up an individually tailored programme, with follow-up visits if required.

# Crying and Comfort

Crying is the only way your baby has of communicating his physical and emotional needs. Some babies cry more than others, but all cry for a reason. Unless your baby is seriously ill he will not keep it to himself. You can give comfort by tuning into his needs and understanding what he wants.

# Crying

Earlier generations of parents were discouraged from comforting a crying baby for fear of 'spoiling' him but we now understand that a young crying baby is not

trying to be manipulative. Research has shown that if you respond quickly to your baby's cries during the first six months, he is more likely to be settled and contented by his first birthday.

### FIRST THREE MONTHS

A baby's body undergoes major changes to adapt to life outside the womb during his first three months. He is establishing feeding, sleeping and waking patterns and many of his vital organs are still maturing, so it's hardly surprising that your baby sometimes seems frustrated and miserable.

- Some experts believe that crying spells in the first year coincide with periods of rapid brain and nervous development at five, eight, 12, 19, 26, 37 and 46 weeks. These are critical times, which researchers have compared to a kind of rebirth.

- Around six weeks tends to be the peak age for crying, when on average most babies cry for up to two hours a day, though some may cry for as many as four hours in any 24-hour period.

- Crying spells tend to diminish at about four months. By the end of his first year your baby will probably only cry half as much as he did during his first three months.

### A DIFFICULT BIRTH

External factors may influence the amount that your baby cries. If he was born after a long or difficult labour, he may cry more and sleep less than a child who had a less traumatic birth (see Cranial osteopathy on page 96). A baby can also be very sensitive to his mother's moods – if you are depressed or anxious you may find that your baby becomes unsettled and cries more frequently.

### COLIC

Colic is a muscular spasm in the wall of the intestines. A baby under three months old who has regular crying spells in the early evening, developing into screaming fits, may be suffering from colic, particularly if he keeps drawing up his legs and appears to be uncomfortable. Colic is not really an illness but more a pattern of behaviour. There are many theories as to its cause, including overfeeding, trapped wind in the digestive tract and tension. Over the counter colic remedies are sometimes helpful, but avoid brands of gripe water containing alcohol. Cuddling, rocking or gently massaging your baby's abdomen (see Baby massage on pages 84–9) are just as effective. Although colic causes a great deal of distress, most babies will outgrow it by the time they are four months old (see Colic on page 100).

### DECODING HIS CRIES

As you get to know your baby you will learn to decode these cries and be able to comfort and console him more effectively.

- A regular, monotonous cry may mean that he is hungry.

- A sharp intake of breath followed by a shrill scream is unmistakeably caused by pain.

- Intermittent grizzling and grumbling lets you know that he is tired and nearly ready for sleep.

# Comforting

Often you will know instinctively why your baby is crying and how to comfort him. Sometimes he will stop as soon as you pick him up. At other times, however, you may be at a loss to calm him and this can be very distressing for both of you. The following are some of the possible causes:

*Hunger*
The most common cause of crying in very young babies, feeding him on demand is the only effective way of dealing with it. Delaying tactics such as offering a dummy or giving him boiled water instead of milk will frustrate him and probably make him cry more furiously.

### Discomfort

He may be too hot or too cold. Ideally he should be kept in a room with a constant temperature of 18–20°C. The best way to check his body temperature is to feel the back of his neck or his tummy. If he feels hot or sweaty remove a layer of bedding or clothing. If he is chilly add another layer. A wet or soiled nappy may also make him miserable, so check and change him regularly. If your baby has a cold, a blocked or runny nose may prevent him feeding and sleeping properly and make him more fractious than usual.

### Tiredness

A very common cause of crying, but one which is not always easy to spot. Trying to comfort a tired baby by picking him up and cuddling him may make him more miserable, not less. He may simply want to be put to bed and left to fall asleep on his own.

### Shock or fear

A newborn baby is very sensitive to external stimuli. Bright lights, loud noises and sudden movements will startle and upset him, as will boisterous play or rough handling. He may also cry if he feels physically insecure. Always hold him gently but firmly so that he doesn't feel as though you are about to drop him.

### Being undressed

Newborn babies don't like being naked, it makes them feel vulnerable and they dislike having their skin exposed to the air. When you are undressing your baby at bathtime or changing his clothes, leave his vest on for as long as possible and when you do take it off, lay a soft towel or muslin across his body.

### Pain

If your baby feels pain, his crying will have a shrill urgent note that will start your adrenaline pumping. The cause may be bathwater that's too hot or an accidental prick with the nappy pin, or he may have a more serious injury. A painful condition such as colic or an ear infection may make him cry inconsolably. If you suspect that your baby is ill, seek medical help.

### Lack of physical contact

Your baby may cry simply because he needs physical reassurance from you. The most natural response to a baby's cries is to pick him up and cuddle him. In many cultures babies are held and carried in slings for most of the time. Hold him close to your body or with his chest and body pressed against your shoulder and walk around with him. If neither of these positions soothes him, try cradling his head and neck in the crook of your left arm so that he is facing outwards, with your left hand supporting his body and your right hand holding him between his legs. Carrying him around in a sling is an alternative way of keeping him close to your body and has the advantage of leaving your hands free. Graduate to a back pack when he's older. Most babies love 'kangaroo care' or skin-to-skin contact with their mother or father. Try giving him a massage (see Baby massage on page 84–9).

Don't let your newborn baby cry for long periods. He will become distraught and it will take you much longer to comfort him if you allow him to become too distressed.

### Boredom

As your baby grows older and becomes more aware of and interested in his surroundings, if he is left on his own with nothing to distract him he will probably cry to attract your attention. Make sure he has plenty to look at when he is on his own. Mobiles (see Homemade toys on page 158), pictures, activity centres and a few favourite toys will keep him amused when he is awake in his cot. Prop him up in his pram or put him in a bouncy chair and let him watch what you are doing.

### Separation anxiety

Around the age of six months, your baby may start to cling to you physically and emotionally. He may become very distressed if he is separated from you, crying even if you are only out of sight for a few moments. Separation anxiety often goes hand in hand with a fear of strangers, he may even become shy with familiar adults. This can be a very trying stage for parents, but it needs careful handling.

Try to get your baby used to the idea of being left with other people, starting with very short periods of no longer than 20 minutes. It's important he understands that when you go out you will always come back. Avoid slipping away without him noticing. He will be distressed if he suddenly finds you are gone and will cry and cling to you even more the next time you try to leave him.

### OH DEAR, WHAT CAN THE MATTER BE...

Even the most contented and settled babies have crying spells. If your baby won't stop crying and you have eliminated all possible physical causes, try:

- repetitive movement. This will remind him of how it felt in the womb. Try walking around with him, rocking him in your arms or in his pram, patting him on the back or on his nappy or even dancing with him.

- sound. Playing music or turning on the television or radio can have a soothing effect provided it is not too loud or strident. Some babies respond to white noise, such as the low hum of a vacuum cleaner or washing machine. Tapes of the sounds a baby hears in the womb are worth trying with your newborn.

- a change of scene. Distract your baby with a trip to the shops or a walk to the park.

- motion. Going for a ride in the car will sometimes calm a crying baby; the gentle vibration and continuous note of the engine seems to have a soporific effect.

- a squeaky toy or rattle. Something brightly coloured which makes a noise can sometimes distract a baby for long enough to forget what he was crying about.

- talking or singing to him softly. Long before he has any comprehension of what you are saying, your baby will find your voice soothing and reassuring.

*Frustration*

Older babies can become very frustrated in they are trying unsuccessfully to complete a task, for example to reach a toy or to sit up. Often you can help them to achieve their objective and this will stop the tears.

### AT YOUR WIT'S END

Most parents have to cope with episodes of inconsolable crying during their baby's first year. Trying to pacify a baby who will not stop screaming when you have tried every tactic you know can leave you feeling exhausted, desperate and even violent. The strength of these negative feelings can be frightening but they are completely normal.

- If you are very stressed your baby will probably pick up on your tension and respond by becoming even more upset. In these situations, the safest thing for both of you is to let someone else take over for a while so that you can calm down, preferably out of earshot of your crying baby. If you are on your own, put him down in his cot, go out of the room and shut the door. He won't come to any harm if you leave him to scream for a little while.

- Living with a baby who cries excessively is an enormous strain and very demoralising. Parents who feel that they are not coping should seek outside help. Some persistently miserable babies respond well to cranial osteopathy (see page 96) or Baby massage (see pages 84–89). Support groups (see Useful Addresses) run helplines and offer advice and information on crying and comforting. Your doctor or health visitor should also be able put you in touch with support or self-help groups.

- Whatever advice is offered by outsiders, never underestimate the power of your own intuition. As your baby grows, you will learn through instinct and experience how best to comfort him. Parents of criers should take heart from the results of a recent study which showed that although mothers' efforts to soothe their babies did not always stop their crying, they did prevent it from escalating into inconsolable screaming.

### COMFORT HABITS

The signficant adults in a baby's life, his mother, father and any other regular carers, provide him with the emotional and physical attention that he needs to feel secure and loved. Comfort habits contribute to your baby's well-being by providing him with another source of reassurance when he feels anxious or vulnerable. They help him to become more independent and develop his inner resources and as long as he doesn't become over-reliant on them you should not discourage them. A happy, well-adjusted child will abandon his comfort habits in his own good time.

### Sucking

This is the most common of all comfort habits and one which often develops at a very early age. Babies are born with a sucking reflex to ensure that they feed. As soon as he is able to find his mouth with his hands, your baby may suck his fingers or thumb for comfort.

### Cuddlies

Older babies often develop an attachment to a special item such as a soft toy, blanket or muslin which they may suck, stroke or simply cuddle. It will accompany them everywhere and they may need to have it with them before they fall asleep. The cuddly's familiar smell and feel is very important and usually the grubbier it is the better. It can be invaluable in helping a baby settle in a strange place.

Keep a spare cuddly in case the original gets lost or irreparably damaged. If your baby has a special cloth cut it in half and put the spare away somewhere safe in case of an emergency.

# Baby massage

In many third world cultures, babies have almost constant physical contact with the adults who take care of them. They may be swaddled and carried around on their mothers' backs or cradled by other family members until they learn to crawl. This period of physical closeness helps the baby adjust to his new environment outside the

## DUMMIES

There is some evidence to suggest that excessive use of dummies may delay normal speech development, but professionals are generally agreed that they are harmless if used only at bedtime and when the baby is distressed. Parents are sometimes concerned that dummies may affect the development of their baby's teeth, but many dentists believe that they cause fewer problems than thumb-sucking, especially if the dummy is orthodontically designed.

*Pros:*
- Very effective at soothing some babies.

- If he has a dummy at night, when he wakes he can suck himself back to sleep.

- Babies who suck dummies rarely suck their thumbs.

- Adults can control dummy use.

*Cons:*
- They can be difficult to give up.

- If he has a dummy at night, he may not be able to find it when he wakes.

- Difficult to keep clean once your baby learns how to put it in and take it out.

- Giving your baby a dummy whenever he cries means that you are dealing with the symptom not the cause.

- Your baby will not be able to explore other objects with his mouth, which is a natural part of his development.

*Dummy safety*
- Sterilise dummies with other feeding equipment during the first year.

- Don't attach it to your baby's clothing. Strings and ribbons are dangerous.

- Check dummies regularly. Throw away any that are perished.

- Never allow your baby to use a bottle of juice as a dummy. It will cause tooth decay and he may choke on the liquid if he falls asleep with it in his mouth.

womb and strengthens the bond between parent and child. In these societies, massage is often a traditional part of newborn care. It is seen as a natural expression of love for the child and has important health benefits, stimulating the baby's immature immune and circulatory system.

### PHYSICAL CONTACT

In the 20th century, babies in the developed world have become physically separated from their parents. From the 1920s to the mid-1960s, childcare theory was parent-centred. Great emphasis was placed on establishing routines and mothers were discouraged from handling their babies. It was common practice for babies to be taken away immediately after the birth to be cleaned and checked over, before the mother could hold her child or put him to the breast. Bottlefeeding was promoted over breastfeeding, and demand feeding, kissing and cuddling the baby were frowned upon in case they 'spoiled' the child.

Childcare experts now acknowledge the importance of close physical contact to a baby's emotional and physical development.

Mothers are expected to feed on demand and are encouraged to hold and cuddle their babies freely.

Massage can play an important part in this early bonding process, providing parent and child with vital skin-to-skin contact in a mutually relaxing situation.

### THE BENEFITS OF MASSAGE

*For you:*
- Helps you get to know your baby and gain confidence in handling him.

- Gives fathers a chance to bond with their babies.

- It's relaxing and soothing for both the giver and the baby.

*For your baby:*
- Fulfils his need for tactile stimulation.

- Has a calming effect if he is anxious or miserable.

- Promotes sleep.

- Helps digestion and circulation.

- Moisturises dry skin.

- Good for co-ordination and mobility.

- Boosts immune system and circulation.

- Reduces colic, constipation, diarrhoea, coughs, colds and irritability.

### WHEN TO START

You can begin massaging your baby from birth. Many babies enjoy just having their head and back stroked to start with. If your baby is happy without clothes you can use a little oil on your hands and massage him naked. If not stroking him with his clothes on will be just as soothing. At around two months, your baby will probably start to enjoy being naked and you will be able massage him more fully.

### MASSAGE OILS

Plant-derived base oils like grapeseed, sweet almond or coconut oil are the most suitable for baby massage. Many commercial baby oils are mineral oils which are not easily absorbed by the skin and tend to block the pores, whereas organic oils allow the skin to breathe. Perfumed products and essential oils should not be used on young babies.

Essential oils can only be used diluted in the base massage oil – three drops of essential oil to four tablespoons of base oil – and only certain oils such as English lavender, teatree and rose, which have healing and soothing properties, are suitable for young babies.

### SAFETY FIRST

- Keep massage oil away from your baby's eyes.

- Don't massage your baby if he is unwell.

- Stop the massage if he cries or seems upset. Try again another time.

- Wait for 48 hours before massaging after an immunisation and avoid the site of the injection.

- Massage can aggravate skin conditions, so take advice from your doctor if your baby has eczema (see pages 123–6).

### PREPARING TO MASSAGE

- Make sure that the room is warm and free of draughts. Small babies lose heat very quickly and your baby will not enjoy being massaged if he feels chilly.

- The best place to massage him is on a soft, clean, cotton surface like a towel placed on the floor, or you can lie him on your lap but make sure your back is well supported.

- Wash and warm up your hands and remove any jewellery in case you scratch or bruise your baby's delicate skin.

- Choose a time when your baby is neither too full nor hungry.

### GIVING A MASSAGE

- Begin by undressing him and placing him on the towel on his back facing you. If he is not comfortable without his clothes on, leave his vest on to start with.

- During the massage maintain eye contact with your baby and talk to him quietly. Keep one hand on him at all times to reassure him.

- Put enough oil on your hands so that they glide smoothly over your baby's skin but not so much that he becomes slippery.

- A five-minute session is probably enough to start with. You can extend it when you become more attuned to his body and he begins to relax and enjoy the experience.

- When you have finished the massage, wrap your baby in the towel and cuddle him before getting him dressed.

*Head*

You don't need oil to massage your baby's head. Using alternate hands, stroke his head from his forehead to the nape of his neck. Then stroke down his cheeks to his chin, taking care to avoid his eyes. Finally, with his head between your hands, use your thumbs to stroke out from above his nose towards his temples.

*Chest and abdomen*

Start at your baby's navel and run your hands over his chest up to his shoulders and down the sides of his body. Using clockwise circular motions, massage his abdomen, working outwards from the navel.

### Arms

Stroke your baby's arm downwards from shoulder to wrist, then gently holding his hand in yours, run your other hand up his arm from wrist to shoulder. Massage the palm of his hand with your thumb and gently stroke his fingers. Repeat with his other arm.

### Legs and feet

Support his heel in the palm of your hand. Massage down your baby's leg from thigh to ankle, using long, sweeping strokes. Stroke the sole of his foot from heel to toe, then stroke each toe individually. Massage the sole of his foot with your thumb using circular motions. Repeat with his other leg.

### Back

Gently turn your baby over and stroke down his back from his shoulders to the base of his spine, making sure that you don't put any pressure on the spine itself. Using plenty of oil, pull his leg hand over hand through your palms. Repeat with his other leg.

# Chapter Four

# Your Healthy Baby

**A**healthy baby is a happy baby so if your baby succumbs to illness in his first months it can be very worrying even if it's just a straightforward cold. Many parents are concerned about giving their babies strong medicines unnecessarily, preferring a natural approach to healthcare. And it is possible for this to be achieved gently but effectively, in conjunction with treatment from your doctor.

## Recognising illness

Mothers will often know instinctively when their babies are ill. They are so attuned to them that they are immediately alerted to any changes in behaviour or appearance. Signs that may indicate your baby is unwell include:

- an unusual or different cry.

- irritable, clingy or whiny behaviour.

- drowsy or sleeping more than usual.

- feeding less than usual.

- vomiting and/or diarrhoea.

- a high temperature or fever – a sign of infection.

- floppy limbs.

- shallow, rapid breathing, fighting for breath or wheezing when breathing out.

- looking paler than usual.

- passing less urine than normal or blood in his nappies.

- a rash.

- glazed, red or sunken eyes.

As you get used to your baby you will learn whether his symptoms warrant just an extra dose of tender loving care, another day to wait and see, an immediate visit to the doctor or an emergency dash to the hospital. However, if you're in any doubt always call your doctor for advice.

## YOUR DOCTOR

A good doctor will support you not just when your baby is ill but with every aspect of his healthcare, so you'll find you spend a lot of time at your doctor's surgery during your baby's first months.

Before seeing your doctor, it's a good idea to make a list of questions or problems you want to talk about. It can be easy to be intimidated by a busy practitioner but it is very important that you understand the advice you are being given and the reasons for the treatment. Don't be afraid to question your doctor or ask about any alternatives. However, remain reasonable and willing to listen, as it is in the best interests of you and your baby to maintain a good relationship with your doctor. Many doctors are happy to consider natural alternatives, providing the baby's health is not being put at risk.

### Your health visitor

Once your baby is ten days old, your midwife will hand over responsibility for his welfare to a health visitor. Health visitors are trained nurses with a special responsibility for practising preventative healthcare. They will carry out regular health checks on your baby throughout his first five years. Do not hesitate to ring your health visitor if you are at all concerned about your baby's welfare – that is what she is there for.

Your doctor's surgery will probably also offer a Well Baby clinic run by health visitors where you can take your baby for his regular health and development checks. An experienced health visitor can be a great source of advice and help as well as someone to talk to about any worries you may have about your baby.

### Examining your baby

A crying, distressed baby is very difficult for the doctor to examine especially after the age of around six months when he's much more aware of what's going on

## Caring for a sick baby

When babies are ill they instinctively turn to the person they know best for comfort. At times like this, no one else will do. You can do a lot to help your baby feel better but it's most important to give him plenty of cuddles and tender loving care.

- Encourage your baby to rest. Sleep is one of nature's greatest healers, allowing the body to concentrate all its energies into fighting off an illness. Babies who aren't given enough time to rest and recuperate are more likely to go down with one illness after another.

- Babies instinctively remain quiet or fall asleep when unwell but they will be most at ease if their mothers are nearby. Carry a young baby in a sling or let an older one sleep in the same room as you during the daytime as well as at night.

- Take your baby out for a walk in a sling or pram so he can sleep and you get a break. It will not harm him to take him out in the car or pram, even if he has a temperature. A change of scene and fresh air will do you both good.

around him. You can make things easier for yourself, your baby and the doctor by appearing as calm as possible. If you are apprehensive, your baby will pick up any tension. If you show confidence and trust in your doctor, so will your baby. Keep him on your knee if possible and if he clings to you, resist your instinct to cuddle him tight. Relax so he knows there's nothing to be afraid of.

# Complementary medicine for babies

Complementary medicine, such as herbalism, homeopathy and osteopathy, is becoming increasingly popular with parents who are looking for safe drug-free remedies to help their children get better naturally. Young children require the gentlest of medicines and natural therapies are oriented towards safe, mild treatments so that many are suitable even for tiny babies. They not only treat the symptoms, they can stimulate the body's own natural healing powers and reduce the possibility of getting the illness

again. And many parents find that when they go to see a practitioner of complementary medicine the opportunity to talk in depth about their baby's problem to someone who seems to listen and care is as therapeutic for them as the treatment is for their baby.

However, it is important to remember that babies and children can become very ill very quickly. Natural remedies, however effective, do not usually give instant results and for acute illnesses and emergencies it is essential to get medical help from your doctor.

### COMPLEMENTARY THERAPIES

The following therapies offer simple and safe treatments for common ailments in babies. This is a very brief guide, so to find out more information about each therapy you will need to consult a specialist book. Most natural health stores and good book shops have a range of books on complementary medicine. Unless you are absolutely sure about a treatment, take your baby to a qualified practitioner for advice first (see Useful Addresses) as there are many natural substances and treatments that may not be suitable and can even be dangerous for your baby.

*Aromatherapy*

Aromatherapy uses essential oils extracted from tiny glands in flowers, stems, herbs, fruits and trees to treat a range of conditions as well as to maintain good health and emotional well-being. It provides a holistic, non-invasive treatment, most commonly through massage, although inhalers, vaporisers and compresses are other aromatherapy treatments. For babies the oils need to be extremely well diluted and can be added to the bath, used in a vaporiser or as a massage oil. The safest essential oils for babies during their first year are chamomile, lavender, fennel, dill, rose and sweet orange. Tea tree, which is generally recommended for problem skin and is very strong smelling, is also suitable but you may prefer not to use it because of the smell.

*Bach Flower Remedies*

These remedies use the healing power of flowers to treat mental and emotional problems. Colour, scent and touch all contribute to the powerful effect of flowers and it is these qualities that Dr Edward Bach developed in the 1930s into a system of healing used all over the world. There are 38 Bach remedies to choose from and all are safe to use for any age with no side effects. Some of the remedies are related to personality types, for example to treat an over-sensitive, fearful baby, and others are used in a specific situation, for example to calm a baby after an accident. By treating psychological problems the remedies can also promote healing of physical symptoms. To choose a remedy you have to be able to assess your baby's state of mind and match it to the right flower essence.

*Herbalism*

Herbs and plants have been used for healing since the earliest times in all cultures. Today, many of the drugs used in orthodox medicine were first derived from plants and still are. There are thousands of herbs and plants each with different properties which have a definite action on a particular body system. Some, such as the lemon, have an antibacterial action or are an antiseptic, such as marigold (calendula). Some, such as chamomile, have relaxant and antispasmodic properties. Only the gentlest and safest herbal remedies are recommended for babies and are best given as an infusion, which is made by pouring boiling water over the herb and leaving for a few minutes. Herbalists use all the therapeutic parts of a plant – flowers, leaves, roots, bark, wood and berries – as they believe it is the plant as a whole that has a medicinal effect.

### Homeopathy

Homeopathy is based on the principle of 'like cures like'. Its origins go back to the fourth-century BC, to the Greek physician Hippocrates, but it was the 19th century German doctor Samuel Hahnemann who developed the idea into the treatment we know today. A remedy using animal, vegetable or mineral substances is prescribed in a very small dose that is known to induce similar symptoms (if used at full strength) to the illness the person is experiencing. This arouses the immune system to overcome the sickness and restore health. The correct remedy can only be selected after careful assessment of the baby or child's mental, emotional and physical symptoms by a qualified practitioner. However there are standard remedies, such as chamomilla for teething, which can be bought over the counter. There are now five NHS homeopathic hospitals around the country.

### Massage

Massage is another ancient therapy and, as well as being good for a baby emotionally, it can be used for treating many conditions from asthma to teething pains. A gentle massage is comforting for babies and the physical contact benefits both baby and parent. Stroking relaxes and tones the muscles, promotes healthy blood circulation and is good for the skin. Massage needs to be gentle but firm using simple strokes and is completely safe (see Baby massage on pages 84–9).

### Osteopathy

This therapy uses gentle manual pressure on the bones, joints, muscles and ligaments to restore proper movement and function. Illnesses can arise when part of the body is out of alignment because it can produce a knock-on effect preventing other organs from functioning properly. Osteopathy can help with many childhood problems from asthma and eczema to colic and glue ear.

### Cranial Osteopathy

Particularly effective for babies and young children, cranial osteopathy is a more subtle approach which involves gently manipulating the skull, shoulders and spine to correct pressures and displacements of the cranial bones and to encourage the flow of cerebrospinal fluid which protects and nourishes the brain. It is used to correct imbalances in the skull caused during the birth and is particularly helpful for excessive crying in babies and for colic.

During the birth process a baby's head changes shape as it passes through the birth canal. The bones of the skull overlap, causing bumps on the head known as moulding. These usually disappear but a difficult birth may leave signs of strain,

which may include:

- Unsettled behaviour and crying to be picked up. Your baby may not find the pressure of a cot mattress on his head comfortable.

- Poor feeding due to head discomfort and compression of the nerves leading to the tongue and throat.

- Ear problems caused by stresses or squeezing during birth.

Make sure you go to a properly qualified practitioner. See Useful Addresses for the National Register which will send you a list of practitioners in your area.

# Common health concerns

As a new parent, it is natural to feel extremely anxious if your baby shows any sign of appearing unwell. Some conditions, like colic or jaundice, may seem frightening but they are common in new babies and will not last long. By following the advice in this section you will help to minimise distress, although you must seek medical advice as indicated.

### NEWBORN JAUNDICE

In the first few days after birth, many babies develop a yellow tinge to their skin – an indication they have newborn or neonatal jaundice. In most postnatal wards you can expect to see at least one newborn 'sunbathing' under special phototherapy lamps. Usually, harmless, neonatal jaundice is caused by a build-up in the blood of a yellow pigment called bilirubin produced by the breakdown of red blood cells in the body and which can't be processed properly by the newborn's immature liver. Around the third or fourth day his skin takes on a yellowish tinge, but within a week or two, as the liver matures, the jaundice clears up naturally.

However, if a blood sample reveals that the bilirubin level is excessively high, there is a very rare possibility that convulsions or brain damage may occur. The treatment involves extra fluids to wash out the excess bilirubin and phototherapy to dissolve the yellow pigmentation in the skin.

While this isn't usually a serious problem it can be very distressing for a new mother trying to get breastfeeding established. Jaundice can cause babies to be drowsy and uninterested in feeding at a vulnerable time when frequent sucking is essential to stimulate milk production.

*What you can do*
- Breastfeed your baby. Your breastmilk is the best medicine he can have – studies have shown that breastmilk is better than water or formula for helping babies get rid of neonatal jaundice quickly.

- Make sure he feeds often so he gets the fluid and calories he needs to flush out the excess bilirubin in his blood. Regular feeds will also boost your milk supply.

- If he's being given phototherapy treatment, don't feel you can't disturb him when he's due for a feed. And don't feel pressurised to get his feed over with quickly so he can get back under the lights.

- If your baby's jaundice is mild, you may be able to treat him at home by putting his cot in natural sunlight near a window. However, you must take extra care that he does not overheat or suffer from sunburn.

### CIRCUMCISION

The surgical removal of the foreskin – the fold of skin that covers and protects the glans (head) of the penis – circumcision is usually now only carried out for religious or cultural purposes. It is rarely necessary for medical reasons and there are no proven health benefits to the operation.

If you are choosing to raise your baby in a gentle, natural way, don't have him circumcised. This is a painful and distressing procedure with the possible risks of bleeding, infection or injury to the penis. Removing the foreskin increases the risk of nappy rash scarring the exposed tip of the penis. However, if circumcision is important to you for traditional reasons, it is strongly advised ythat you have the operation done under local anaesthetic by a doctor.

### COT DEATH (SUDDEN INFANT DEATH SYNDROME)

Sudden infant death syndrome – the unexplained death of an apparently healthy baby – is the biggest fear of all new parents. Although it is rare, occurring in one in 700 children usually in the first six months and peaking between two and four months, it is still the biggest killer of children under a year old. No one yet knows for sure what causes it but by taking the recommended precautions you can significantly lower the risks.

*What you can do*
- Put your baby on his back to sleep. Evidence has shown that this is the safest position to sleep in, as it prevents babies from burying their faces in the mattress and becoming overheated. Lying face down can cause the upper airways to become obstructed too. Don't worry that your baby may choke in this position, even babies born at 34 weeks have a well-developed gag reflex which means they will cough to prevent milk from going down into their lungs. It is also advisable

to put your baby to sleep with his feet touching the bottom of the cot so he cannot wriggle down under the covers.

- Make sure your baby doesn't overheat (see page 52 and Healthy sleeping on page 71). Keep the room temperature at 18°C and no hotter. Do not let your baby wear a hat indoors. Don't throw an extra blanket over the cot at night if you have left the central heating on, as babies sleeping in a warm room with too many clothes or blankets may be vulnerable to cot death. You will know if your baby is too hot if he is sweating, has damp hair or is restless. If he is hot remove a layer of bedding. Remove hats and extra clothing as soon as you go inside, even if it means waking your baby.

The Foundation for the Study of Infant Deaths provides the following guidelines to the amount of bedding your baby needs, assuming that he is wearing a vest, nappy and sleepsuit. Never let your baby sleep with a hot water bottle or electric blanket, next to a radiator, heater or fire, or in direct sunshine. Duvets, quilts, baby vests, sheepskins and pillows may carry a risk of overheating. If the room or air temperature is 15°C, cover him with a sheet plus three to four layers of baby blankets; at 18°C, use a sheet plus two to three layers of baby blankets; at 21°C, use a sheet plus one blanket; at 24°C, use a sheet only. Remember, a folded blanket counts as two blankets.

- Don't smoke and don't allow your baby to be exposed to cigarette smoke. All researchers agree that smoking is one of the main contributors to cot death: if both parents smoke, the risk of cot death is five times higher than if neither parent smokes. Smoking during pregnancy also increases the risk of babies being born prematurely or with breathing problems which can make them more vulnerable to cot death.

- Breastfeed your baby (see Breastfeeding on page 8). The natural way to feed your baby has clear advantages: breastfeeding even for a short while reduces the likelihood of infections which may affect breathing but, if he does get an infection, his airways are less likely to be as congested as a bottlefed baby's. Because a breastfed baby is more likely to sleep close to you and wake more frequently than a bottlefed baby, you may be more attuned to his breathing patterns and be able to pick up any difficulties.

- Sleep in the same room as your baby. For the first six months when your baby is most vulnerable, keep his cot in your bedroom. A New Zealand study published in *The Lancet* in 1996 has shown that babies who share the same sleeping room as one or more adults have a lower risk of cot death (SIDS) than babies who do not share (see Whose bedroom? on page 71).

- Contact your GP if your baby seems unwell. Many cot death babies have been shown to have had minor respiratory infections. If your baby is under six months old and has a temperature of 38°C for more than two hours, speak to your doctor. If he doesn't improve, or seems to get worse, contact your doctor again even if it is the same day or night (see Fever on page 109).

- Choose the right cot mattress. Scientists have claimed that cot death may be caused by toxic gases given off by chemicals in mattresses. This research is controversial and has not been accepted by Government scientists. If you want to avoid the slightest risk buy a new mattress for each baby and check it doesn't contain the fire retardants antimony, phosphorous or arsenic (see Safety first on page 144).

## COLIC

When an otherwise healthy baby cries regularly and inconsolably during the evenings for no obvious reason during his first three months, colic is usually the cause, especially if he keeps drawing his legs up over his tummy. Feeding may stop the crying but only temporarily. No one yet knows the cause of colic or how to cure it, but this muscle spasm in the intestine is thought to be linked to the baby's immature digestive system and possible culprits include wind, cow's milk, tense mothers, parents who smoke and, according to some researchers, even emotional problems in the baby.

*What you can do*
- Check your baby's feeding position to make sure he's not taking in too much air. Feed him in an upright position and don't lie him down immediately afterwards. Wind him halfway through as well as when he's finished. If you're bottlefeeding, experiment with a teat with a different sized hole. Some new babies have a milk flow that is too strong, whilst older babies may need a bigger hole to increase the flow.

- Try and relax when you're feeding – use the breathing exercises you learned at antenatal classes if you find it difficult. Sensitive babies can pick up the nervous tension of an anxious mother.

- If you are breastfeeding, consider your diet. Try cutting out dairy products, spicy or garlicky foods, or caffeine for a few days only to see if this improves the colic. Feeding little and often may be easier on your baby's digestion.

- A colicky baby may want to suck your finger, a dummy or a bottle of tepid water rather than take in extra milk which he is not digesting properly.

- Don't smoke and don't allow smoking in your home. Researchers have found that nicotine transferred into the mother's milk can upset a baby, as can cigarette smoke.

- Try holding your baby in different positions when he's crying and rocking or walking with him.

- A warm bath followed by a massage, concentrating on the abdomen, may ease the pain (see Baby massage on pages 84–9).

- Take your baby to be treated by a cranial osteopath (see Cranial osteopathy on page 96).

If nothing helps, you can only reassure yourself that the colic will eventually subside, usually when your baby is around three months old, and will have no lasting effects on him. However, if he seems ill between bouts of colic and is not gaining weight, take him to your doctor.

- Over-the-counter products such as Infracol help to break down any large air bubbles and should be given before feeds.

*A natural remedy*

Make your own 'gripe water' by simmering one teaspoon of dill or fennel seeds in one pint of water for 10 minutes. Strain and cool then give to the baby on a spoon.

Trials in Germany have shown that chamomile can be effective in relieving infantile colic. Mix one teaspoon of dried herbs in a cup of boiling water. Cool and give to your baby – up to three cups a day. Alternatively, add 5-10 drops of chamomile oil three times a day to a little warmed water or milk.

## IMMUNISATION

Immunisation is designed to protect both individual children and the community from infectious diseases that can cause serious illness and death. These illnesses are measles, mumps, rubella (German measles), whooping cough, polio, tetanus, diphtheria, haemophilus influenza Type B (HIB), which is one of the causes of childhood meningitis, tuberculosis and hepatitis A and B. However, immunisation is becoming more and more of a dilemma for parents who want to do the best for their baby but are concerned about the possible side effects of the vaccines. Is it worth facing the risk of catching a disease rather than have the immunisation?

*How do vaccines work?*

Vaccines work by giving a healthy child a mild form of an infectious disease. This stimulates the body to produce antibodies against the germ without causing the disease, enabling the baby to develop an immunity which will fight off the disease if he is exposed to it later on. Sometimes the effects of the vaccine wear off so a booster is required.

*What are the risks?*

Doubts about the vaccines have arisen after formerly healthy children have become chronically ill after immunisation or gone into anaphylactic shock (severe allergic reaction). An increase in allergies, worsening of asthma and eczema, recurrent ear infections and learning disabilities have all been linked to immunisation. Recently the measles vaccine has been associated with autism and Crohn's disease, a disorder of the bowel. However, serious side effects from immunisation are very rare and research has shown that the risks of harmful effects from the diseases themselves, such as blindness, deafness, paralysis, brain damage or death, are far greater. Between 1978 and 1989, 25 million children were immunised among whom 118 anaphylactic reactions were reported.

*How is it done?*

Your child will receive five sets of vaccines during his first five years, starting at around two months. Most are injected, apart from polio which is given by drops placed on your baby's tongue. However, if he is unwell beforehand, immunisation can be postponed. Most children suffer no reactions to the vaccines but possible mild side effects include a raised temperature, soreness at the injection site, a rash and irritability.

Reasons not to have your child immunised at all are:

• If he has had a severe reaction to a previous injection.

• If he has had a severe allergic reaction to eggs (MMR – measles, mumps and rubella vaccination – may not be given)

• If your child has a serious, malignant disease like cancer.

*Homeopathic vaccines*

There are no proven effective alternatives to immunisation. The Council for the Faculty of Homeopathy strongly supports the immunisation programme, using the conventional tested vaccines, unless there are medical reasons not to have your child immunised. In this case, you may choose to consult an experienced qualified homeopath to boost your baby's natural immunity.

## TEETHING

Some babies may show signs of suffering as their new teeth push through their sensitive gums from the age of five to six months. Your baby may become irritable and cry more if his gums are sore. He may also become more clingy and wakeful at night and dribble and develop sore red skin around his mouths and cheeks.

*What you can do*

- Chewing can bring relief. Give your baby something firm to chew on such as a piece of apple of carrot, but beware of choking. A teething ring cooled in the fridge can also be effective.

- Teething gels containing antiseptic and analgesics may be recommended for babies over four months. Calpol, a paracetamol solution, relieves severe discomfort.

- The homeopathic remedy chamomilla, available as teething granules, can give effective relief and is a natural alternative to anaesthetic teething gels.

- Never assume that if your baby is unwell it is due to teething. Fever, diarrhoea, vomiting and ear infections are not symptoms of teething so always see your doctor.

## DENTAL CARE

By the age of two and a half your baby is likely to have all his milk teeth. These first teeth are precious – they will be needed for eating for years to come and they keep the growth space for permanent teeth.

*What you can do*

- Start cleaning the teeth morning and night as soon as they come through (see Cleaning teeth on page 61).

- Use a fluoride toothpaste. Toothpaste helps remove sugar, food, plaque and bacteria from the mouth. Fluoride strengthens the developing enamel which surrounds teeth, making it more resistant to decay. Flouride drops which can be given from birth up to the age of four, are also available. If you live in an area with added fluoride in the water, check with your dentist whether you should give your baby fluoride toothpaste and supplements. Excess flouride can cause fluorosis – a condition which causes mottling and discoloration.

- Sugary drinks and food are teeth's worst enemy. Restrict sweet drinks to mealtimes and offer water if your baby is thirsty between meals. Try to get your baby used to savoury snacks as treats.

- Don't give your baby juice in a bottle. Sucking on a bottle teat keeps the teeth constantly bathed in juice and is known to cause bottle caries. As soon as he's able, encourage the use of a trainer cup for all drinks.

- Look out for hidden sugars in food and drinks. Dextrose, fructose, glucose and maltose, although all natural sugars, will rot the teeth. Be especially careful with pure fruit juice – it should be very well diluted for babies and children.

- Continue breastfeeding. Studies have found that one of the best contributors to good jaw alignment which helps prevent dental decay later on is a baby's sucking action on the breast.

*A natural remedy*

Chamomile is the best natural remedy for soothing sore gums. Add one drop to an eggcupful of cold water and stir. Dip a cottonwool bud in the solution and gently rub your baby's gums. Store in the fridge for 24 hours and use when needed.

# Common childhood illnesses

All babies are susceptible to certain illnesses, as their immune systems do not contain sufficient antibodies to fight off infections. If your baby is ill, keep him with you during the day and night so you can check on him frequently. Ask your partner to take turns if the illness lasts more than a night or two as you will need some uninterrupted sleep to cope with looking after a sick baby.

Babies can become ill quite quickly, developing a fever and sometimes getting very lethargic. If this happens it is important to wake them regularly. Remember that each illness helps to build up their resistance for the future.

## INFECTIONS

Breastfeeding your baby will help ward off infections during the first few months but it's only a matter of time before he picks up one bug or another. Most infections don't give cause for concern unless they are accompanied by a high fever (see Fever on page 109) – tender loving care and time are the greatest healers. However, you will probably need to consult a doctor, especially when your baby is under six months.

Infections are caused by viruses or by bacteria. A virus attacks the body by invading a cell where it replicates itself many times. Each of the new copies then finds its own host cell and repeats the process. Bacteria live in and on the body and many don't cause disease, in fact some are beneficial. Harmful bacteria cause disease when they are present in large quantities. Antibiotics will be your doctor's biggest weapon against bacteria but they have no effect on viral infections.

## COLDS

The most frequent ailment of babies and toddlers, colds are caused by viruses which infect the lining of the nose, sinuses, ears, throat and bronchi in the lungs. Symptoms are a runny nose, sneezing, sore throat and cough. There is no cure for the cold but there are a range of remedies you can try to make your baby more comfortable. If you are worried about your baby or he is unable to feed, seek medical advice.

## Preventing infection

Even the healthiest babies are likely to catch the odd cold during the first year but there are measures you can take to reduce the likelihood of your baby picking up an infection.

- Breastfeed for as long as possible. One of it's many benefits is that it helps defend the baby against infections. Breastmilk destroys harmful bacteria and contains antibodies passed from the mother that protect him from infections. Breastfed babies are less likely to suffer from respiratory and urinary infections, ear infections and gastroenteritis. If a breastfed baby does pick up a tummy bug, he will recover much more quickly because he is able to continue feeding, unlike a bottlefed baby who may not be able to tolerate formula milk.

- Give your baby a healthy diet. Eating fresh, natural foods which provide all the essential nutrients will help him to be more resistant to infection (see Weaning on page 28).

- Don't smoke and don't allow smoking in your home. Studies show that babies exposed to cigarette smoke have a much higher incidence of ear infections, bronchitis and sinus infections.

- Where possible, try to keep your baby away from anyone with an infectious illness.

- Sterilise feeding equipment for the first few months and once your baby starts putting everything in his mouth keep his toys clean, particularly if he has been 'sharing' them with other babies.

*What you can do*

- Keep him comfortably warm but not too hot. Taking him out for a walk in the fresh air may help to relieve his symptoms and distract him from his discomfort.

- If his nose is red and sore a dab of petroleum jelly such as Vaseline will protect it. If you prefer a natural remedy try calendula or chamomile cream.

- Offer plenty of drinks – either cooled, boiled water, well diluted pure fruit juice or breastmilk – little and often to prevent dehydration.

- For babies over three months you can try a natural decongestant, such as eucalyptus oil, available from the chemist. Put a few drops on your baby's sleepsuit – the natural vapours may help improve your baby's breathing. Alternatively, use a vaporiser – there are some which use tablets of essential oils.

- Raising the head of his mattress slightly will help prevent a blocked up nose at night. Place a pillow under the mattress at the head end.

- Don't be tempted to dose your baby with infant paracetamol every time he has a cold; save it for when he really needs it, for example when he has a fever (see Fever on page 109).

*A natural remedy*
Add three drops of eucalyptus essential oil to a bowl of boiling water and leave near your baby's cot but out of his reach. The vapours will help relieve his symptoms.

## COUGHS

Usually following on from a cold, a cough is the body's natural way of clearing excess mucus and phlegm from the breathing passages. However, if your baby has a dry, tickly cough it is usually caused by inflammation in the throat and lungs and may be a reaction to irritants in the atmosphere.

If your baby is eating and sleeping well there is usually no cause for concern but coughs can sometimes be a symptom of a more serious problem. If the cough lingers and your baby also sounds wheezy, it may be due to an allergy such as asthma or if it comes on suddenly and persistently, your baby may have swallowed something which has become lodged in an airway. With either or these, seek medical advice.

*What you can do*
- Your baby's cough may sound distressing but it is actually serving an important purpose clearing the airways. A 'productive' cough brings up mucus and phlegm and reduces the number of germs moving towards the lungs. This type of cough should not be treated with a suppressant medicine as it will prevent it from serving its protective purpose. However, if you feel you want to help nature take its course, an expectorant medicine is designed to loosen the secretions so they can be coughed up more quickly and easily. Some doctors doubt whether children's cough medicines have any effect – apart from making parents feel they are doing something to relieve their child's discomfort.

- There are some foods which increase the production of mucus and encourage a cough to linger. Cow's milk, cheese, sugar and bananas should be avoided during and for a week or two after a cold or cough.

- Give your baby plenty of drinks to soothe his throat and help loosen the mucus.

- Don't expose him to the cold because if he becomes chilled this can make a cough worse and cold air hitting his airways will also aggravate the cough.

- Don't allow smoking in your home – cigarette smoke will aggravate his cough.

*A natural remedy*
One teaspoon of honey and of freshly squeezed lemon juice in a cup of cooled, boiled water may help soothe his cough.

## FEVER
Parents don't usually need a thermometer to tell if their baby has a temperature – instinct and a hand on the forehead are enough to alert them that their child is not well. However, if you're unsure or you'd prefer to know how high it is, a forehead

indicator strip or a thermometer held in the armpit will give you a rough indication. An accurate temperature can only be obtained using a rectal thermometer but it is rarely necessary to use this invasive method.

### HOW TO REDUCE A FEVER

- Make sure your baby is not overdressed, and remove blankets leaving only a sheet.

- Open a window to let in cool air.

- Give extra fluids to prevent dehydration – breastmilk or cooled, boiled water will help.

- A lukewarm bath may help but don't put him in a cold bath – he will hate it and may start to shiver which will send his temperature back up. Alternatively, sponge him with tepid water. Don't dry the skin afterwards as the natural evaporation of the water has a cooling effect.

- Give infant paracetamol following the dosage instructions on the label.

A baby's normal temperature is between 36°C and 37.5°C and anything above is considered a fever. However, the degree of the fever doesn't necessarily match the severity of the illness. Other signs of fever include flushed cheeks, fast heartbeat, breathing faster and sweating.

A high temperature or fever is usually an indication that the baby has an infection and the body is trying to combat the bacteria or virus causing it. Although it doesn't necessarily indicate a serious illness, babies under six months should always be seen by a doctor. Other cautionary signs are if your baby develops a rash, is floppy and lethargic, vomiting, drowsy, pale, not feeding, or crying inconsolably or very weakly. Fortunately, most babies with a fever quickly respond to infant paracetamol, increased fluids and cooling down.

*Febrile convulsions*
It is important that you get your baby's temperature down quickly as some children between the ages of six months and five years are prone to febrile convulsions or 'fits'. These occur as the result of a sudden

## MENINGITIS

A high temperature or fever is one symptom of meningitis, an infection of the membranes lining the outer surface of the brain. Viral meningitis is less serious but bacterial meningitis is potentially fatal, especially in babies, and urgent medical attential is essential. Each year there are around 1800 reported cases of bacterial meningitis in England and Wales, but this figure is now falling because of the success of the HIB vaccine. The three types of bacterial meningitis are meningococcal, pneumococcal and haemophilus influenza type B (HIB). The germs that cause bacterial meningitis are very common and live in the back of the throat. People can carry them for weeks without becoming ill. Only rarely do they overcome the body's defences and cause meningitis. Meningitis can also be caught from water supplies and swimming pools. Recognising the symptoms could mean the different between life and death. Meningitis develops quickly within a few hours. If your baby also has any of the following symptoms seek help immediately:

- high pitched, moaning cry

- persistent vomiting

- increasing drowsiness

- an aversion to bright light

- purply-red rash or bruises: this can occur anywhere on the body and is due to blood poisoning

- stiff neck

- bulging fontanelles – the soft areas on a baby's skull before the skull bones fuse together.

Not all these symptoms may appear together.

*Meningitis test*
If your child develops a rash anywhere on the body, press the spots or bruises with a glass or your finger. If they do not turn white, meningitis should be suspected.

rapid rise in temperature which irritates the brain, causing the child to become unconscious, his body to become rigid and his limbs to jerk. When the convulsion is over, usually after a minute or two, cool him down and call the doctor. Fortunately, though very frightening for the parent, these fits do not cause any lasting harm.

*A natural remedy*
Syrup of elderflower and peppermint, available from health shops, is a good children's remedy for fever.

### CROUP

Croup, signified by a harsh, barking cough along with laboured breathing, can follow on from a cold and cough or it may begin without warning. It is caused by an acute infection of the larynx (voice box), or trachea (windpipe) resulting in inflammation of the airways, reducing the amount of air reaching the lungs and making it difficult for your baby to breathe.

There are two types of croup: viral croup most commonly affects babies and although it can sound quite frightening it is usually only a mild illness with a slight cold and fever which may last for a few days. However, bacterial croup can be more serious. Attacks usually occur at night and if a child has great trouble breathing, large swings in temperature, refuses drinks and is obviously distressed, seek medical help immediately.

*What you can do*
- During an attack of croup try and calm your baby because if he is frightened and crying this will aggravate the croup. Breastfeeding may help or you can try cuddling and carrying him or looking at books together.

- Steam treatment is the traditional and most effective method of clearing his breathing passages. Sit with him in the bathroom, close the door and windows and run the hot tap into the bath with the plug in to create a humid atmosphere. Or use an electric kettle – but don't leave your child alone even to phone the doctor.

- Offer cold drinks to reduce inflammation.

- At mealtimes during the day when he's not having an attack, just give him well-puréed foods to minimise the risk of choking.

- If he has a fever, give him infant paracetamol to help bring his temperature down.

- If you can't ease your baby's symptoms call a doctor.

*A natural remedy*
The homeopathic remedy aconite is recommended for a dry, barking, croupy cough. Give one dose of the 30 c potency, then a second half an hour later.

### EARACHE

One of the most common childhood complaints, earache is usually caused by a viral or a bacterial infection. If after a cold your baby becomes hot, miserable, crying and clingy particularly at night, vomits and keeps pulling at his ear or his face, you can suspect otitis media – inflammation of the middle ear. It is a painful condition due to a build-up of fluid trapped in the middle ear which presses against the eardrum and is worse when lying down. Sometimes the pressure causes the eardrum to burst and the fluid leaks out which often relieves the pain. Ear infections are diagnosed with an otoscope (viewing instrument) so you must take your baby to the doctor who will prescribe a course of antibiotics, even though the infection may be caused by a virus (see Antibiotics on page 126). If otitis media is left untreated, it can cause damage to the ear cavity or bones within it leading to permanent hearing loss. It is essential to complete the course of antibiotics even though your baby may make a quick recovery or the infection is likely to return. Have your baby's ears checked a couple of weeks later to ensure the fluid has completely cleared.

Earache can also be caused by inflammation of the outer ear canal (otitis externa) or by poking something into the ear, tonsillitis or an injury to the ear.

*What you can do*
- Give infant paracetamol to ease the pain.

- Wrap a warm hot water bottle in a soft towel and cuddle your baby with it against his ear.

- Avoid exposure to cold winds.

*A natural remedy*

Put a piece of cottonwool soaked in slightly warm (not hot) extra-virgin olive oil into the ear. Make sure the cottonwool is big enough so that it cannot be pushed right inside. Add one drop of lavender and one drop of chamomile essence, if you have them, to one teaspoon of olive oil. Mix well and soak cottonwool in the mixture.

### STICKY EYE

Soon after birth many babies get a yellow discharge in one or both eyes caused by a blocked tear duct. The tears can't drain properly and accumulate in the eye in a sticky pus. Though the eyes aren't sore the pus may stick the eyelids together when the baby is asleep. There is also a risk that the discharge may become infected. Blocked tear ducts almost always clear themselves by the first 12 months.

*What you can do*

- Wipe away the pus frequently using cooled boiled water and cotton wool.

### REDUCING THE RISK OF EAR INFECTIONS

Recurrent ear infections can lead to problems in the future such as glue ear or hearing loss. The following measures may help lessen your baby's susceptibility to ear infection:

- Breastfeed for as long as possible. Research has proved that breastfed babies have fewer ear infections due to the protective effects of breastmilk.

- If your baby has food allergies, particularly to dairy products, he may be more likely to get ear infections. Dairy products encourage the production of mucus which can cause a build-up of fluid in the middle ear. Consider swapping to soya or goat's milk but if you are bottlefeeding check with your doctor, health visitor or a nutritionist first.

- Your GP may prescribe decongestant nose drops to clear the catarrh.

Wipe from the inside of the eye outwards and use a separate piece of cotton wool for each eye.

- With scrupulously clean fingers and very short nails, gently massage the tear ducts in the inside corner of your baby's eyes. If done regularly several times a day this can help to clear the ducts. If they haven't cleared themselves after six months, consult your doctor.

### CONJUCTIVITIS

A red, sore or itchy eye and inner eyelid with a greeny-yellow discharge in older babies usually indicates conjunctivitis, an infection of the delicate lining covering the outer eye and inner eyelid. Your baby is likely to rub his eyes, passing the infection from one to the other.

*What you can do*
- Unless you are sure your baby's red eye is due to conjunctivitis see your doctor to check the soreness is not due to an injury.

- Clean away the discharge from the eye

with a piece of cotton wool soaked in half a teaspoon of sea salt dissolved in a cup of cooled, boiled water. Use a new piece for each eye and wipe from the inner to the outer corner of the eye.

- If you are still breastfeeding, use a little freshly expressed milk to bathe the eyes.

- Conjunctivitis is highly contagious so always wash your hands after treating your baby and use a separate flannel and towel for him. Change the sheet on his mattress every day.

- If the eyes haven't begun to clear after three days see your doctor. He may

prescribe antibiotic treatment to clear the infection.

*A natural remedy*

To soothe sore or red eyes make a solution with five drops of tincture of eyebright (from health shops) and one cup (240 ml) of cooled boiled water. Soak some cotton wool in it and wipe his eyes as described above, using a new piece for each eye.

### VOMITING

All young babies regularly bring up a little of their feeds, known as possetting, and this is nothing to be concerned about, as long as the baby is healthy, feeding well and gaining weight. Babies may also be sick if they take in too much air when they feed and regurgitate milk along with the wind. Bottlefed babies who bring up a lot of milk after every feed may be allergic to or intolerant of the formula and you may need to change to another formula in consultation with a nutritionist or your health visitor.

Vomiting, when the contents of the stomach are brought up forcefully, is usually triggered by toxins caused by an infection such as gastroenteritis but it can also be a symptom of ear and throat infections as well as more serious illnesses including appendicitis, pneumonia and meningitis.

Vomiting isn't usually serious and passes within a few hours though it may be followed by diarrhoea. Dehydration – loss of body fluids – is the biggest worry and in the most severe cases can cause death. If your baby is vomiting persistently it is essential to see a doctor to find the cause. Medical conditions that also may be responsible include pyloric stenosis, hiatus hernia and coeliac disease.

Another possible cause of vomiting in older babies is accidental poisoning from medicines, household chemicals or plants. If you suspect your baby has swallowed something toxic, you should seek urgent medical attention.

*What you can do*

• Vomiting is unpleasant and frightening for a baby, so he'll need lots of tender loving care. A bout of vomiting can be exhausting so let him lie down and rest afterwards.

## VOMITING
### – WHEN TO GET HELP

- If the vomiting has lasted for more than 24 hours.

- If there are signs of dehydration: a dry mouth and lips, sunken fontanelles, infrequent urination or dark, concentrated urine, sunken eyes, drowsiness, lethargy.

- If the vomiting follows a fall or head injury.

- If the vomiting is accompanied by other symptoms and you are concerned.

<br>

- If you are breastfeeding, continue to feed him if he wants to but don't give him formula milk. Cow's milk is likely to make him vomit again. If you are bottlefeeding, offer your baby clear fluids for 24 hours (see oral rehydration below). Contact your doctor if he is not able to keep this down. Introduce milk at half-strength for the next 24 hours before returning to full-strength formula feeds.

- Offer cooled boiled water, a little at a time in case it is brought back up. Keep offering this to prevent your baby from becoming dehydrated (see Vomiting – when to get help).

- You can also give him an oral rehydration solution available from the chemist. This dissolves in water to replace the correct balance of salts and sugars lost by vomiting and to help prevent dehydration. Offer it frequently in small amounts from a bottle or teaspoon or for older babies you can freeze the solution in lolly moulds for them to suck.

- Don't give him solid food or formula milk until the vomiting has subsided for 24 hours. When his appetite returns offer bland, puréed food to start with.

*A natural remedy*
Ginger is an effective remedy. Give one teaspoon of ginger root in one cup (240 ml) of boiled water. Strain, cool and add honey.

## DIARRHOEA

The term diarrhoea refers to the consistency of the stools rather than how frequently they are passed. The number of times babies pass motions varies widely – breastfed babies may pass stools after every feed or there may be three or more days between a motion. If your baby has diarrhoea, his stools may be liquid, green, mucus-containing, foul-smelling or blood-tinged. He may have a sore red rash around the anus.

### Acute diarrhoea

A sudden attack usually due to gastroenteritis, acute diarrhoea is usually the result of a viral infection, although food poisoning may be responsible. When the intestinal lining becomes infected, it's unable to absorb nutrients from food in the digestive process and allows it to pass through rapidly, resulting in frequent, watery stools. If the infection also causes vomiting and fever, there is a risk of dehydration, particularly in a young baby, and in this situation medical attention is essential.

### What you can do

- See your doctor if you are at all concerned about your baby, particularly if he is showing signs of dehydration.

- Replace lost fluids with cooled, boiled water or a rehydration solution (see Vomiting, page 116).

- Breastfed babies can continue to feed as normal as human milk is not irritating. Even if the baby vomits his body will absorb some of the nutrients. However, cow's milk formula and dairy products should be avoided as they will prolong the diarrhoea.

- Don't withhold food unless your baby is vomiting as well. If he shows signs of wanting to eat give him a little bland food such as banana, mashed potato, rice or porridge made with water. As he improves slowly return to his normal diet, saving dairy foods till last.

- Don't give your baby drugs to dry up the diarrhoea. Diarrhoea due to infection is part of the body's response to invading bugs and helps to flush them out of the bowel. These drugs slow down the action of the intestines and can in fact worsen the condition because the germs and infected fluid stagnate in the gut, protracting the course of the illness.

- Always wash your hands thoroughly after changing a nappy to avoid spreading the infection.

### Chronic diarrhoea

When the condition persists in a mild form or comes and goes, it may be due to a medical condition such as cystic fibrosis, coeliac disease (a wheat intolerance) or Hirsch prongs disease (dilated colon). In all three conditions your baby will have very pale, smelly stools which float and are difficult to flush away, indicating that the body is not digesting fat properly. Or it may be a result of an intolerance to dairy products or a side effect of a course of antibiotics. Intususception, a condition where the bowel gets stuck within itself, causes diarrhoea and the passage of blood in the stools (known as 'redcurrant jelly' stools), as well as vomiting and colic.

### What you can do

- Determine the cause. One of the most important things to establish is whether your baby is gaining weight normally. If he isn't, or is losing weight and appears unwell, see your doctor urgently. If he appears to be well, his diet may be causing the loose stools.

- If you think a food intolerance is responsible, try cutting out the suspect food for a week or so to see if there is any improvement. Then give your baby the food again to see if the diarrhoea recurs. Consult your doctor, health visitor or a nutritionist before making any major changes to his diet.

- Avoid high fibre or whole foods such as raw vegetables, brown bread and brown rice until your baby is older and better able to digest them.

- Check how much fruit juice your baby is drinking. Too much juice, particularly apple, is known to aggravate diarrhoea. Always give fruit juice that's been well diluted.

*A natural remedy*

For both chronic and acute diarrhoea, add two drops of lavender essential oil to four tablespoons of almond base oil and massage into your baby's abdomen in a circular clockwise motion (see Baby massage on pages 84–9).

## CONSTIPATION

If your baby is obviously suffering discomfort while straining to pass a stool, which is hard and pebble-like, he is constipated. However, he is not necessarily constipated if he passes motions infrequently, since frequency varies greatly between babies, depending on age and diet. It is usually due to insufficient fluids or a poor weaning diet, which cause hard, dry, hard stools that are difficult to pass. Sometimes streaks of blood can be seen on the outside of the stool, caused by a tear in the lining of the rectum. This will be painful for your baby, making him reluctant to pass stools, exacerbating the problem.

*What you can do*

• Try and find the cause of the constipation. If you have just changed your baby's diet, for example introduced weaning foods or switched from breast- to bottlefeeding, this is a likely cause.

• Give your baby more fluids to drink, either water or well diluted pure fruit juice. Prune juice or diluted freshly squeezed orange juice are both good remedies for constipation.

• Avoid foods which may contribute to

## SAFETY FIRST

• Keep all medicines out of reach, ideally in a locked medicine cabinet

• Keep by the phone a list of emergency numbers: doctor, hospital accident and emergency, local police and late night chemist.

• Go on a first aid course to boost your confidence and skills in an emergency – the Red Cross runs ones specifically for parents and carers of babies and children.

constipation such as unripe bananas, cow's milk, cheese and eggs. Instead offer more fresh fruit and vegetables which contain natural fibre.

- Don't use suppositories or laxatives except as a short-term solution if recommended by your doctor.

*A natural remedy*
Massage is the safest treatment for constipation in babies. Gently stroke your baby's lower abdomen in a clockwise direction (see Baby massage on pages 84–9).

# Allergies

Eczema and asthma are closely related allergic conditions – babies with eczema are three times more likely to develop asthma than other children and in 70 per cent of cases there is a family history of allergic illnesses. Eczema, also known as dermatitis, affects around 15 per cent of babies and young children, although fortunately most grow out of it as they get older. The number of children with asthma has doubled over the last 20 years and it now affects one in seven children in Britain, many of whom will also grow out of it.

## ASTHMA
Symptoms, which include wheezing, coughing and breathlessness, usually start to occur after the first year, though from six months babies can develop a persistent nighttime cough. Often caused by an allergic reaction to substances such as house dust mites, pollen, animal dander or food, asthma occurs when the sensitive linings of the airways in the lungs (bronchial tubes) are irritated, swell and go into spasm, restricting air flow. The linings may then leak mucus which further clogs up the air passages, making coughing and wheezing even worse. Babies under a year may get bronchiolitis which has similar symptoms to asthma but is caused by a viral infection. Recurrent attacks may lead to asthma later on as can frequent colds or catarrh. Any baby with a cough that does not respond to antibiotics should be monitored for asthma.

If you suspect that your baby may have asthma or similar, it's essential to take him to your doctor for a correct diagnosis, although doctors may prefer to 'wait and see' before labelling a baby with such a chronic condition. Your baby may grow out of his symptoms or they may be due to some other illness.

*What you can do*
If you feel your baby may be at risk from asthma, follow these guidelines to reduce his susceptibility:

- Breastfeed your baby for as long as possible as bottlefed babies are known to be more vulnerable to asthma.

- Don't allow smoking in your home.

- Try and reduce contact with common allergens such as house dust mites, feathers, moulds, pollens and pet fur, which can irritate the linings of the respiratory passages and trigger an attack (see Indoor pollution on page 134 and Eczema triggers on page 125).

- Try not to buy soft toys as they harbour dust mites. If your baby must have a teddy or soft toy, kill off the mites by once a week putting it in a plastic bag, leaving it in the freezer overnight, then defrosting it and washing it at 60°C.

- Diet can sometimes be a factor. Food additives, especially yellow dyes, sodium benzoate and sulphates are a trigger. Ask your doctor if you should try cutting out mucus-producing foods, especially dairy products such as cow's milk and cheese. Give foods that are easy to digest. Some babies are affected by refined sugar while others react to food additives.

- Spray your child's mattress with dilute lavender or tea tree essence (two drops to half pint/300 ml) to kill dust mites each time you change the sheets.

- If your child does develop asthma he will usually need drugs to control the attacks. However there are various natural therapies (such as aromatherapy, homeopathy, herbalism or naturopathy) you can use at the same time to help prevent attacks from occurring. Take your child to a practitioner of complementary medicine for advice.

*A natural remedy*

A thyme bath can benefit a wheezy baby. Make an infusion of 2–3 teaspoons of thyme in boiling water. Leave it to stand for five minutes then pour into the bath water.

### ECZEMA

Eczema is an itchy, sore-looking rash which may be reddened, dry, scaly, bleeding or weepy. There are many forms of eczema but the two types that usually affect babies are a form of seborrhoeic dermatitis (cradle cap) and atopic eczema. The cause of the eczema can be very hard to pinpoint but is thought to be triggered by allergens similar to asthma. There is no cure, though there are treatments that can alleviate the symptoms.

*Cradle cap*

Caused by overactivity of the sebaceous glands which lie at the root of the hair follicles, cradle cap can be mild with just a few flaky patches on the top of the head or severe with a greasy thick yellow crust all over the scalp. Fortunately, it rarely distresses the baby and clears up on its own when the skin naturally becomes drier.

*What you can do*

• Massage a little olive oil into the scalp before bedtime to soften the patches. Wash your baby's hair the following morning, gently rubbing off loose scales. Never pick off the scales as the scalp may become infected.

• Always use a mild shampoo and rinse thoroughly.

*A natural remedy*

After washing the hair rinse the scalp with a decoction of burdock root, which has been shown to have antibacterial, antiseptic and antifungal properties. Place the burdock root in a saucepan, pour on water, bring to the boil and simmer for 10–15 minutes before straining. Do not use an aluminium pan. Use one tablespoon of root to one pint (600 ml) of water.

*Atopic eczema*

Atopic eczema often starts as irritating, dry, flaky patches on the face when a baby is

though complementary practitioners believe that childhood eczema is linked to the digestive system.

*What you can do*

- Eczema is very irritating and it will be hard to stop your baby from scratching, particularly at night. Keep his nails trimmed to minimise the damage to his skin. Light cotton mittens will also help but many babies hate wearing them

- Use emollients, available on prescription, to keep the skin moist and soft. These can be creams or lotions to apply directly to the skin or liquids to add to the bath water. They help prevent the skin from dryness which can cause itching and further inflammation.

- Avoid using soap or perfumed bubble baths.

- Your doctor may prescribe a mild steroid cream. This should only be used for a very short time during a flare-up. Long-term use of strong steroids can cause side effects including skin damage but these

aged between three and six months, although breastfeeding can help delay its onset. A rash then spreads to the scalp, neck, skin creases and nappy area. It also occurs on the joints such as the backs of knees and around the elbows and ankles. The rash is intensely itchy and the skin may be reddened, cracked and thickened. Scratching can cause bleeding and infection.

The exact cause of eczema is not known

## ECZEMA TRIGGERS

- If you have a family history of allergy it is wise to try and avoid food allergens for the first year. These include cow's milk, eggs, orange juice and wheat. Food additives, colourings and preservatives can also cause a reaction. If you suspect that certain foods may be triggering your baby's eczema try cutting each one out for a week and noting any effects. However, consult a nutritionist before radically altering his diet on a long-term basis.

  If you are breastfeeding try cutting out cheese, cow's milk, red meat, greasy foods or rich and spicy foods for a week or two to see if any of these have an effect on your baby.

- Avoid irritants likely to inflame your baby's skin. Dress your baby in pure cotton clothes next to his skin and avoid wool and synthetic fibres in clothes and bedding. Biological washing powders, fabric conditioners, perfumed soaps, bubble baths and shampoos should be avoided.

- The house dust mite is another known culprit. (see Indoor pollution on page 134). If you suspect your baby is reacting to dust wash bedclothes frequently in a hot wash or use an allergy-proof cover on the mattress and duvet (if he is old enough for one). Don't put wool blankets on the cot. Remove furry toys from the bedroom or give them the freezer treatment (see Asthma on page 121). Keep the bedroom cool and open the window daily to improve ventilation. Vacuum frequently but not with your baby in the room. Damp dust regularly. Get rid of dust-collecting clutter in his room.

- Furry pets may also produce an allergic reaction – the skin scales (dander) they shed are a strong irritant. Don't allow cats or dogs in your baby's bedroom.

should not be prescribed for babies. Mild steroids, like 0.5-1% hydrocortisone will not cause skin damage on babies if applied as prescribed.

- Orthodox medicine has little to offer eczema sufferers but natural therapies have been shown to be very beneficial. Medical trials at Great Ormond Street Hospital have found Chinese herbs to be very effective. Always see a professional practitioner before treating your baby.

*A natural remedy*
Two to three drops of Bach Flower Rescue Remedy (available from health shops) added to the bath may help relieve pain and itching.

# Antibiotics

Parents are becoming increasingly anxious about the use of antibiotics, particularly if they are trying to bring up their baby in a safe and natural way. While there is no doubt that antibiotics play a vital role in fighting life-threatening diseases such as meningitis and pneumonia, their

inappropriate or repeated prescription is giving rising cause for concern among some medical experts and scientists. Antibiotics work by killing or stopping the growth of bacteria that cause infections. Though they may be effective in the short term they have a number of side effects and can even cause recurring bouts of the illness.

### Side effects
- Nausea. The toxic effect of the drug on the body can cause nausea.

- Diarrhoea. Antibiotics can disturb the balance of bacteria in the digestive tract and cause diarrhoea.

- Thrush. Antibiotics can encourage the secondary infection of thrush to develop in the mouth or genital area.

- Allergic reaction. Some babies may develop a rash a few days after starting treatment.

### Causes for Concern
- Antibiotics can appear to cure an illness in the short term, only for it to return later, possibly in a more virulent form.

This creates a vicious circle of infection and antibiotic use. If doctors aren't sure about the cause of an illness they often 'play safe' and prescribe an antibiotic. They may also prescribe antibiotics unnecessarily for illnesses they can't treat such as sore throats, colds, coughs and some forms of chest infection, such as bronchiolitis.

- Overuse of antibiotics has meant that some infections that used to be easy to treat are now difficult to cure, as the bacteria responsible have become resistant to the drug by making genetic changes to themselves. This has resulted in some antibiotics becoming ineffective. Superbugs have developed that are resistant to four or more antibiotics so the infections they cause are particularly difficult to treat.

- Antibiotics may not only kill harmful bacteria but also the helpful bacteria that inhabit our bodies. This upsets the body's natural equilibrium and allows a new infection to develop. For example thrush is a fungal infection that is usually kept in check by helpful bacteria but often develops after a course of antibiotics. Some research has linked outbreaks of meningitis with overuse of antibiotics.

*What you can do*
- Give the antibiotics as prescribed and complete the course even though it's tempting to stop as soon as your baby seems better. Antibiotics kill off the most susceptible bacteria first, leaving the most resistant. If you stop giving them halfway through the treatment, you leave behind the stronger bugs which cause a recurrence of the symptoms.

- Give your baby acidophilus powder (available from health shops) daily during the course of the antibiotics. This may help to restore the normal bacteria in the gut that are killed by the antibiotics.

- If your doctor doesn't feel urgent medical attention is required, try a natural remedy. They all work at boosting the body's immune system so it will do the healing work.

# CHAPTER FIVE

# The Natural Home

**H**ome is where the memories of childhood are made. Once you have a baby you will certainly spend more time in your home and the 'nesting instinct' that so many parents experience may inspire you to take a fresh look at where you live and to consider ways of adapting it to suit the needs of a growing family. You may decide to redecorate a spare room as a nursery, or you may feel you need to plan an extension or even a complete house move.

## Where you live

If you are considering moving to somewhere more spacious to accommodate your growing family you may want to weigh up the relative benefits of town and country living.

### IN TOWN

The advantages of living in a town are:

- Good public transport. As your child grows up and becomes independent, he will be able to get himself to and from school and friends.

- Access to parks where children can play safely. Most parks have a fenced-off playground.

- Sports centres, creches and other facilities are more common in built-up areas.

- A healthy diet. Recent research suggests that, contrary to what most people believe, children brought up in towns enjoy a healthier diet than country-raised children. Parents have access to a wider range of fresh fruits, vegetables and alternatives to high-fat foods.

- More social opportunities. Research has shown that mothers of young babies in towns are less isolated, with more opportunities to mix socially at toddler groups and organised clubs.

The disadvantages are:

- Air pollution. Cars, the major source of air pollution, pump out a toxic cocktail of pollutants which can cause breathing difficulties, reduce resistance to infection, aggravate asthma and even cause cancer. Babies and children are particularly vulnerable to pollution because they are growing. Their bodies are generally quicker to absorb substances and slower to eliminate them, according to environmental pressure group, Friends of the Earth.

- Young children pushed in buggies along pavements next to busy roads are at face level with exhaust pipes which pump out the fumes.

- Busy roads also mean that there is an increased danger of accidents.

- Lead pollution is undoubtedly higher in towns. Lead is a poisonous metal. Contact with it can lead to anaemia, high blood pressure and damage to the nervous system in young children. Low-level lead pollution, from fumes and lead piping (see What about water? on page 26) can impair the mental development of babies and toddlers without symptoms.

### IN THE COUNTRY

The advantages of living in the country are:

- Better air quality. Although in the spring and summer there is a greater risk of hay fever due to higher levels of pollen.

- Fewer cars, so if you live in a village you may feel it is safer to allow your children to walk and play unsupervised outside the home once they reach a certain age. In the UK road accidents involving children have dropped by a third over the last 10 years.

- If you are keen to live in a house built from natural materials from the local environment (see below), you will probably find a greater choice in a rural area.

- Closer contact with nature. Your children will see animals in the fields, crops growing, fruit on trees. They will enjoy walks with you across fields and woodland areas.

- Larger garden. Generally houses built in rural areas have more generous garden space, which will be useful as your baby grows into a toddler and can enjoy sandpits and slides.

The disadvantages are:

- Limited public transport. Traditionally country living conjures up a picture of healthy children, but recent evidence suggests otherwise as children have to be driven to school and their friends are usually more spread out. The average child today walks 50 miles a year less than he did 10 years ago and travels 40 per cent more miles by car (3,158 miles in 1992 compared with 2,259 miles in 1985) and it is country children particularly who have become more sedentary.

- Sports and other facilities are often far away.

- Risk of being isolated with a new baby. Isolation of new mothers has been linked to postnatal depression, a serious condition that affects up to one in 10 women after the birth of a baby.

### COUNTRY MATTERS

If you decide to bring up your baby in a rural area, check if it has a reasonable train and bus service. This is also important if you are planning to return to work. Once your baby is born you may want to join in activities in the village so, if there is a community centre, it would be worth moving to where you will have easy access to it.

Some schools are starting to promote safe routes to school in association with local police forces. Again you can check where this is happening in the area that interests you. If your baby is not yet born this may sound a long way off, but those first four or five years will pass very rapidly and you may find that, once you have put down roots in a certain area, you will be loath to move on.

### WHAT'S IN A HOUSE?

Traditional building materials, such as bricks, stone and wood, provide a healthy framework in which to live and bring up your baby. But in our quest for comfort, we have introduced all sorts of chemicals into our homes with potentially serious consequences. In Britain the term 'sick building syndrome' has been coined to describe a repeated illness caused by the buildings in which the sufferers live or work.

Materials which provide cause for concern include:

- Hydrocarbons and other solvents. Commonly found in adhesives, paint strippers and wood treatments, these poisons have been linked to birth defects when either the mother or the father has been exposed to them, according to Brigid McConville, author of *The Parents' Green Guide*. Keep your baby well away from the fumes if you are using solvents while redecorating your home. Never put old paint strippers down the drain, as they upset the balance of the bacteria which decompose sewage.

- Cavity wall insulators. These can reduce heat loss by half. If you are having cavity wall insulation installed, don't use one containing formalin and formaldehyde.

Make sure that the skin containing the insulation is not cracked, allowing fumes to leak into the house. The insulator Micafil is free of these chemicals.

- Formaldehyde. As well as being used in the UK in insulating foam, this potent irritant is found in synthetic varnishes, plywood glues, chipboard, hardboard, wallpaper, fabric and carpet finishes. Formaldehyde seeps slowly out of the materials into the home. It can cause headaches, depression and dizziness, as well as affecting the eyes, nose, throat and lungs. Choose natural wood kitchen and bathroom cupboards and fittings if you can.

- Asbestos. Known to cause lung cancer, the use of asbestos as a building material is now banned, but if you are renovating an old home you may come across it in pipe lagging and boarding. Contact your local Environmental Health Officer immediately if you suspect you have found asbestos.

- Plastics. The manufacturing process of

## ECOLABELS

To help you decide, look out for products awarded an Ecolabel. This scheme is a voluntary environmental labelling scheme for consumer products set up by the European Union in 1992 and designed to help consumers select, and to encourage manufacturers to make, products which do less damage to the environment.

Each country must establish a competent body to run the scheme; in Britain, it is the UK Ecolabelling Board. Air contamination, noise, consumption of energy, effects on the environment and consumption of natural resources are some of the criteria used for judging different products. So far washing machines, dishwashers, toilet paper, detergents, lightbulbs, bedlinen, paints and varnishes and fridges are just some of the products to have been awarded Ecolabels. For more information, contact the UK Ecolabelling Board on 0171 820 1199.

plastics pollutes the environment and some plastics, including PVC, pollute the atmosphere of your home once they are in place. In household fires more people die from the effects of toxic fumes as furniture is burned than from the fire itself. Don't buy plastic chairs and sofas.

- Paint. Modern paints are less toxic than the old-fashioned varieties and the use of lead has been banned in Britain since 1986. But if you move into an old home that has not been decorated since then, there may be traces of older, more dangerous, lead paint. Lead can impair children's mental ability, so don't sand down old paint while your baby is nearby. Make sure that all paint is dry, the fumes have evaporated and the room is fully aired before you allow your baby into a newly painted room. Paint manufacturers have been working towards less harmful products. An example of this is lowering the content of Volatile Organic Compound (VOC). But beware of choosing a paint containing titanium dioxide, used as a pigment for white paint; the paint industry admits that the energy used for producing this pigment, and the resulting emissions, are major polluting factors.

  You can use toy safety paints for skirting boards and areas your baby is likely to come into close contact with. Also, look out for paints awarded the Ecolabel, such as Dulux and Crown gloss paints. Take care when throwing away leftover paint or paint scrapings. If your local authority does not operate a special chemical waste disposal service, wrap them up securely and put them in a dustbin.

- Wood treatments. Lindane and dieldrin are commonly used as woodworm killers but both are toxic and lindane has been linked to leukaemia.

- Wood. If you want to help preserve the environment and reduce the destruction of the world's rain forests (100 acres are being cleared each minute) avoid buying household furniture that uses tropical hardwoods like teak, mahogany, ramin and iroko. Choose the faster growing softwoods pine, larch and spruce.

- Ducted air heating. As air is recirculated, some experts believe that dust and bacteria are simply breathed in again and again.

Building contractors are now starting to introduce passive ventilation, a new system which puts draughts back into buildings. It brings fresh air from the outside into internal rooms, allowing fresh air into the atmosphere and stale air a means of escape. Heat recovery is another new system that can even out the heating in your home, transferring heat from a warm room into a colder one.

### INDOOR POLLUTION

- Cigarette smoke is one of the greatest indoor air pollutants. Smoking near your baby dramatically increases the risk of him contracting bronchitis, asthma and pneumonia or being a victim of cot death (see Your Healthy Baby on pages 99 and 107). In a household where 20 or more cigarettes are smoked each day, a baby is eight times more at risk of cot death, according to the Foundation for the Study of Infant Deaths. Babies and children in households where parents smoke are forced to inhale dangerous quantities of nicotine and carbon monoxide, making them passive smokers. Mothers who smoke while they are pregnant increase the chances of suffering a miscarriage and producing a low birthweight baby. Your baby is twice as likely to develop childhood cancers if you smoke. Foresight, the organisation for the promotion of pre-conceptual care, recommends that both parents should stop smoking four months before trying to conceive a baby. Smoking damages sperm, which take about 12 weeks to form. Remember, sperm are responsible for half a baby's genetic makeup.

- Wood and coal fires can pollute the atmosphere if the flue is not adequate or regularly cleaned. Gas fires can also leak into the home if they are not fitted correctly by a registered fitter.

- House dust mites live in the dust that accumulates in carpet, bedding, fabrics and furniture. They thrive in warm, wet conditions so use an extractor fan in bathrooms, open windows and doors regularly and try not to dry washing on radiators. Up to two million mites can live in one mattress. Each mite will lay 40 to 80 eggs and produce 20 faecal particles a day during its 10-week lifespan. These droppings, which are easily blown around and inhaled, are a major irritant for allergy sufferers (see Allergies on page 121). Repair any sources of damp, such as water leaks and rising damp, and make sure your tumble dryer is vented externally. Dust surfaces with a damp cloth and vacuum thoroughly (see Vacuum cleaners on page 136)

- Pets shed particles of skin and fur, called dander, which contain allergens produced by the animal's sweat glands that can cause asthma, eczema and hayfever symptoms. Cat allergens,

particularly, can remain in a house for years after a cat has lived there. If you have a cat, encourage it to sleep on a special blanket in a basket and wash its bedding regularly to limit the spread of its dander. Keep cats away from your baby's sleeping area.

*Air ionisers and filters*
Air filters are claimed to filter pollutants out of the air and ionisers clear the air by electrically charging the particles. There is little medical evidence to suggest that they are essential to the natural home. Keep fresh air circulating in your home by opening windows and doors instead.

## HOUSEHOLD AIDS

More and more domestic appliances and equipment are being developed with the environment and our health in mind. For example, since the end of 1994, no new CFCs have been produced in Britain and other countries within the Economic Union. There have also been agreements to reduce the quantities of used and recycled CFCs imported into the EC.

Furthermore, manufacturers are now realising that consumers are interested in saving energy. Fridges, freezers, washing machines and cookers all vary tremendously in the amount of energy that they consume. Choose a washing machine that uses less detergent and water than other makes and a fridge without CFCs in the insulating foam.

*Fridges*
If you are choosing a fridge, always look for a model that uses hydrocarbons (Hcs) in the refrigeration circuit and the insulating foam because they do not contribute to ozone depletion, unlike the the traditional CFCs. The manufacturers should also supply an instructions manual on how to use the fridge in an environmentally friendly way.

*Vacuum cleaners*
Some vacuum cleaners are designed with high levels of filtration to recirculate less dust. High suction power and low levels of dust in the exhaust are important if you want to reduce the risk of spreading house

dust mites around your home. Manufacturers claim that some models are better at reducing asthma symptoms but there has been no medical research to prove this. Remember to change the dust bag regularly – look for a model with a self-sealing or sealed dust bag to minimise spreading house dust in the atmosphere during disposal. The Dyson Absolute has no dustbag with dust being emptied straight from the collecting bin. This means allergy sufferers have to handle the dust.

*Cooking equipment*
Choose stainless steel, cast iron or enamelled cookware rather than aluminium

## Saving energy

One kilowatt of electricity provides roughly two hours of vacuuming, three gallons of hot water or two hours of ironing. But its production also causes 10.1 grams of sulphur to be emitted into the air by power stations. This eventually falls as acid rain, affecting our health and damaging buildings and wildlife.

Save energy by:
- not overheating your house. Young babies need to be kept warm, but many of us overheat our homes. Keep the temperature at about 18°C and no higher than 20°C.

- using low-energy lightbulbs. These last for nearly a year and use 80 per cent less energy than conventional bulbs. A good lighting shop should stock them.

- keeping your hot water temperature at a reasonable level with a thermostat. Scalding hot water that needs a lot of cold water added is wasteful and a safety hazard to young children.

- turning off the lights when you leave a room.

- fitting wall cavity insulation (see What's in a house? on page 131).

- buying low-energy white goods (see Household aids on page 136).

cooking pans. Although they are more expensive, they are long-lasting and safer. Recent research suggests there may be a link between the aluminium in our diets and the increase in the incidence of Alzheimer's Disease in adults.

A pressure cooker is a good energy-saving investment. It enables you to cook complete meals at once and by steaming vegetables at the top of the pan, you can ensure your baby receives all the nutrients that are often destroyed by traditional boiling.

### RECYCLE YOUR RUBBISH

- Our society produces a frightening amount of rubbish. Each of us creates up to 10 times our body weight in waste each year! In Britain 7.7 million tons of paper and cardboard are used each year – 5 million tons of this are thrown out.

- Set up systems for recycling as much household waste as you can. With a new baby in the home you may be buying new equipment which will be heavily packaged. Now is a good time to organise separate bins for leftover food and vegetable peelings, glass bottles and jars, metal cans and a box for paper and card (nearly 30% of our rubbish is paper and card). Local authorities and supermarkets provide bottle banks and collection points and some local authorities arrange for paper to be collected along with household rubbish.

- As your baby gets bigger and outgrows his clothes and toys, you can take them to charity shops or hospitals. Tattered clothing can be recycled too and some local authorities provide textile banks at collection points. As your child grows up he will learn to conserve resources too, if he sees you setting an example.

# Car travel

Once you have a baby, you may need a car that's comfortable, roomy and convenient for family travelling. A spacious boot is vital to store your baby's pram, pushchair and all the other equipment you will need to travel with for the next few years. Hatchbacks are easy to access and some estate models have a third row of seats that can convert to extra boot space. If you are planning to have more than one baby, extra seat capacity will be useful once you are ferrying small children and their friends to playgroup and other activities. Sharing journeys also cuts down on pollution and helps to conserve petrol.

### LEAD-FREE PETROL

Lead-free petrol reduces the amount of lead pollution in our atmosphere and a catalytic convertor, fitted on all new cars, also helps to reduce the amount of toxic material emitted from the exhaust. Try to choose a model which is economic to run and does not gobble up petrol by the gallon. Although diesel is more efficient, it still produces toxic emissions and so is best avoided.

If you have a secondhand car that still uses leaded petrol, you may be able to have it converted at low cost. Check with your garage.

### IN THE CAR

Making sure your baby is safe when you travel in the car is vital. You need to have a car safety seat or a properly anchored

### SAFETY FIRST

When buying a car, consider these points:

- Check for child safety locks on doors and windows and avoid models with heavy, sliding doors that could trap little hands. High seats enable even babies to see out of the window and enjoy long car journeys.

- If you choose a jeep-style car avoid the models with bull bars fitted to the front. These have proved to cause more injury and fatalities in accidents involving small children.

- Many new cars are now fitted with airbags which inflate in a collision to protect people in the front seats. American-made cars have been fitted with higher-powered airbags and in the US small babies strapped into the front seat have been killed by the force of the expanding balloon. Don't put your baby in the front seat if you own a car which has an airbag fitted.

carrycot even before you bring him home from hospital. There is a wide variety of car restraints available:

- Carrycot. You can use this on the back seat with child restraint straps that are fitted on to the frame of the car. Once your baby starts to pull himself up, change him to a car seat.

- Rear-facing infant carrier/baby safety seat (birth to nine months). This is a lightweight inexpensive seat with handles that makes it easy to transport your baby in and out of the car. You can also use it to sit him up in at home. It buckles into

### CHOOSING A CAR SEAT

When choosing which seat to buy, consider:
- how easily the harness adjusts.
- whether the covers are machine washable.
- whether the seat reclines.
- how well it supports your baby's head.

an adult safety belt and can be used on the front or back seat. It faces backwards so that, in the event of an accident, any pressure is exerted against the baby's back rather than his pelvis, which is still too soft to protect the internal organs properly. However, if your car is fitted with airbags, only use this carrier on the back seat (see Safety first on page 139).

- Front-facing car seat (nine months to four years). Once your baby can sit unsupported you can use a front-facing car seat. Choose one with wings to provide head support . Many models can be adjusted into a reclining position, which is useful if your baby wants to sleep. These seats are generally high enough for him to see out of the window and some have clip-on trays. Some car seats span both age ranges.

- Booster seat (four to 11 years). Again your child can look out of the window and is raised to a proper height to enable him to be properly restrained with an adult seatbelt.

### BELT UP

Anchorage kits can be bought from both babycare and specialist motor parts shops. If you are not sure whether the seat you have bought needs a specially fitted anchorage kit, ask the shop assistant for advice or contact one of the advice helplines run by car seat manufacturers and car safety organisations.

The RAC reports that more than half of child seats are fitted incorrectly and four out of 10 parents in the UK are not using car restraints at all. If you don't feel happy about fitting the kit yourself, you can get it professionally fitted at a garage.

To make sure your baby is properly strapped in:

- check that the seat buckle is not resting on the metal frame.

- shake the seat before you put your baby in. If it moves more than two millimetres you need to tighten the fittings.

- adjust the harness on every journey to take into account what your child is wearing.

### CAR POLLUTION

Cars are the major source of air pollution in the UK today. Environmental organisations like Friends of the Earth are campaigning for people to walk or cycle instead of driving if it is safe to do so and for more use to be made of public transport.

There is a limited amount that you can do to avoid the effects of the pollution but you can help by:

- Keeping informed about air quality. The Department of the Environment runs a Pollution helpline and calls are free.

- Whenever possible leave the car at home and ask friends and family to do the same.

- Get involved with Friends of the Earth and other campaigning organisations (see Useful Addresses on page 188).

- keep the harness buckle as low as possible, so the lapstrap rests on your baby's hips and thighs and not his stomach.

# The nursery

When you first step into a babycare shop, you may be overwhelmed by the amount of equipment on display – cots, Moses baskets, bouncy chairs, highchairs, car seats, playpens, safety gates, rows of toys, clothes and feeding accessories – all designed to look as appealing as possible and all threaten to carve a huge dent in your bank balance and swamp your home.

### PLANNING AHEAD

Make sure you buy only the essentials by planning ahead:

- Ask friends and relatives with babies what they found most useful and which makes lasted well. The most expensive items of nursery equipment are not always the best.

- If you are planning to have more than one baby it is worth paying more for

goods that will remain in reasonable condition.

- Find out which items were a complete waste of money – there are all sorts of unnecessary gadgets on the market – and don't be pressurised into buying them.

### PREPARING THE NURSERY

Your young baby will be happiest sleeping in your room for the first few months of his life and you will quickly get to know his sleep and breathing patterns if he is close by (see Bedtime on page 69). If you have a spare room for him to move into later on, you may find it helpful to have it ready before he is born. It will be a useful place to store his clothes and equipment.

- You will only need the bare essentials – a chest of drawers for his clothes and nappies, a clean surface for baby lotions and toiletries and a sturdy box or basket for toys.

- Try not to clutter up his room with too many ornaments and knick-knacks. Although these look pretty, they serve little purpose and your growing baby will not understand the difference between toys that he is encouraged to play with and precious ornaments he can't touch.

- Clutter also increases the risk of accidents. As your baby becomes mobile, it is important to keep floors as clear as possible of furniture with sharp edges and too many toys. When he starts to pull himself up and 'cruise' around the furniture, he will be able to grab all sorts of objects that you thought were safely out of reach.

- Painting the walls of the nursery rather than papering them makes it easier to smarten up as your baby grows older and grubby hands and crayons leave their marks. There is a wide choice of stencils and friezes available to use as decoration and as your baby grows into a toddler, you can start to display his first works of art, too.

- Some children are allergic to the chemicals in paints. If you are concerned, use water-based rather than solvent-based paints.

- Although a soft carpet looks appealing and comfortable for a baby to sit and play on, it is not the most practical as it will collect dust – and house dust mites (see Allergies on page 121 and Indoor pollution on page 134) – and the inevitable spillages, such as baby lotion and milk, may be difficult to mop up. You may prefer to choose cork tiles or vinyl instead.

- Washable roller blinds will attract less dust than Venetian blinds or curtains and a natural wicker nursery chair is preferable to a padded one.

- Strip lighting or adjustable spotlights are more practical than a lamp with a pretty shade, another dust collector. Make sure the light is not directly above your baby's cot where it will shine straight into his eyes.

- Your baby's room should stay at a constant temperature of about 18°C.

During very cold weather you may need to adjust the heating so it stays on during the night at the right setting to maintain this temperature. A room thermometer may help you assess how warm the nursery is. If you don't have central heating, you will need a convector heater that conforms to safety standards. These will cut out automatically if they are knocked over and some can be wall-mounted.

### YOUR BABY'S BED

You will need somewhere for your baby to sleep. He won't be fussy, so long as it is comfortable and secure with a safety mattress that has air vents at the end his head will be. A wicker Moses basket with a hood to keep out draughts and protect his eyes from direct light will be suitable, as will a pram or a carrycot which fits into a pushchair. At around three months, you will need to move him into a cot. Some have adjustable bases, so that you can raise the mattress for ease of access and gradually lower it as he learns to pull himself up on the cot bars. Many cots also have a drop-side mechanism, so you can lower one side to lift your baby in and out and change the bedding. (See also Bedtime, Chapter Three).

### BEDLINEN CHECKLIST

All cot bedding should be flameproof:

- cotton sheets – stretch terry or cotton glove sheets fit best.

- cotton cellular blankets – light, warm and easy to layer.

### SAFETY FIRST

- Make sure that the handles of the Moses basket or carrycot are robust and they distribute your baby's weight evenly when it is picked up.

- Fit a foam mattress which has air holes to allow your baby to breathe if he rolls on to his front when he is asleep.

- Cots are expensive but safety standards have improved in recent years. Some models will convert into a child-sized bed which will last for a number of years.

- Choose a cot with bars set at gaps of no more than 6.5 cm. A larger gap is dangerous as your baby may get his head stuck between them or his body may fall through and trap his head.

- Check that the mattress conforms to safety standards BS 1877 and BS 7177 and make sure that it fits snugly. A gap of more than 4 cm is unsafe as your baby might trap his head between the mattress and the side of the cot. Check also that it is firm and smooth – it should mould to your baby's shape.

- Don't use a cot more than 15 years old. The spacing of the bars might be too wide and old paint finishes and varnishes may not conform to current standards of toxicity.

- Don't choose a drop-side cot with a large screw at the top, which could catch your baby's clothing. As he gets bigger, make sure he cannot operate this himself.

- Make sure the paint is non-toxic and that there are no transfers on the inside where the baby can reach them.

- Adjust his layers of bedding to ensure that your baby sleeps at a constant temperature.

## BABY MONITORS

### Listening monitor

Many parents find that a two-way listening monitor brings peace of mind. One unit is placed in the baby's room and the other is fully portable and can be carried from room to room and, with some models, into the garden on a special belt clip. The monitor can be set to record your baby's every sound or just to pick up louder sounds like crying. Some even have a nursery light attachment on the unit in his room.

If this gives you the confidence to sit and watch TV without worrying that you will not hear your baby cry it's a worthwhile investment. But you may prefer to keep your baby close to you, particularly in the first few months. It will probably be more comforting for him as he has been used to background noise and the sound of your voice while in the womb. You will also be able to tune in to his sleep patterns and reactions more easily.

### Breathing monitor

A baby breathing monitor is a sophisticated

device with small sensors or pressure pads that are placed on the baby's stomach to detect the tiniest change in his breathing pattern. Parents should only use one under supervision and if they have been trained in resuscitation. Unless your baby has a serious health problem or there is a history of cot death in the family, a breathing monitor will be unnecessary.

### BABY TRANSPORT

There is an enormous range of baby transport available. You need to think carefully about your lifestyle and what type of equipment would best suit it before you part with your money. For example, if you live in an upstairs flat you may decide that a pram is impractical and opt for a baby sling and fold-away pushchair combination. On the other hand, if you expect to do a lot of walking, a sturdy pram with high sides to protect your baby from wind and rain may be the best choice. You can choose from:

- A pram with detachable body. The carrycot can be used separately and the chassis folds down for storage. Check that the handle is at a comfortable height for pushing and that you can carry the carrycot separately if you need to.

- A three-in-one pushchair. This combines a pram and carrycot with a pushchair and will take you through until your baby is at least two years old. Check whether the pushchair seat is adjustable so that it reclines back and is suitable for a young baby.

- A stroller or buggy. A lightweight, folding pushchair, which is easy to store and carry. You can buy a hood and apron to protect your baby from wind and rain. Check that the seat is wide enough to last as your baby grows and whether it will recline. You also need to find out at what age your baby can first go into it, as some are not strong enough to support the back and head of a newborn.

- A pushchair. A basic one-position pushchair is a useful spare or extra to keep at the grandparents' house or in the boot of the car. Check if you can buy a hood and apron to go with it.

- A baby sling. Useful for carrying your young baby inside and outside the house, leaving your hands free. He will love the warmth and security of being snuggled up to you. The head support can be removed once your baby gains head control. Check that the sling is easy to put on unaided and that it sits at a comfortable level on your body. These can cause back and shoulder ache when worn for long periods of time, particularly as your baby gets bigger.

### TRANSPORT EXTRAS

- A shopping tray fits underneath your pram or pushchair and will store shopping much more safely than a bag dangling from the handles.

- In bad weather, a hood and apron will keep your baby warm and dry as they seal him off from inclement weather.

- A 'cosy toes' muff will keep your baby's legs warm. Only use in cold weather.

- A pram net will protect your baby from animals and insects in the summer.

- A canopy or parasol will protect him from the sun (see Fun in the sun, pages 181–6).

- A backpack. Once your baby is about six months old, a backpack enables him to watch the world go by. Check that it is adjustable and has padded shoulder pads and belt for comfort. It should also have an adjustable seat for added comfort too.

### Safety straps

All forms of transport should be used with a harness once your baby is two months old and tiny babies should always wear a harness if they are put in a reclining pushchair. Get into the habit of using them on every outing, however short.

### SITTING UP

From about three weeks old, your baby will enjoy sitting and watching your movements

## Buying a highchair

- Safety. The highchair must feel stable. As your baby grows he will enjoy leaning over the side. The highchair must be strong enough to remain stable at all times. It must also have harness points. Check for gaps that could trap little fingers.

- Ease of use. Consider how easy it will be to lift your baby in and out of the chair and how easy it will be to clean. A removeable, plastic tray is useful – it should have a contoured edge to stop pieces of food or the plate from dropping over the edge. You will have to clean the seat and legs regularly too, as food is bound to spill.

- Comfort. Some chairs have padded seats or you can buy a specially moulded cushion that fits into the highchair seat for added comfort and security. This is particularly useful when you first start using the highchair and your baby is still small.

for parts of the day. You can either use a baby safety seat (see In the car on page 139) for this or a baby bouncing cradle, which you can also rock. This will last your baby until he is about four months old, when you will need a more solid seat with better support.

NEVER put your baby's seat on a table or raised surface and always strap him into his seat, even if you only plan to leave him in it for a few seconds.

When your baby is about six months old you can put him in a highchair. It's worth taking time and trouble to buy one that you are happy with, as you will be using it several times each day until your baby is about two years old. There are several types available:

- Folding highchair. This folds flat like an ironing board and can be stored out of the way when not in use. It's useful if you are short of space but it can be tedious to have to put it up each time you want to feed your baby, particularly if he is desperate for food! The legs are often widely splayed and can be a safety hazard as you work around your baby.

- Convertible highchair. Often made of wood, this is the sturdiest and most comfortable highchair. Later it will convert to a low chair and table so when your baby gets to toddler stage he can sit at it to eat or draw.

- Standard highchair. With wipe-clean surfaces and detachable tray, this usually has metal legs. Some models convert from a low chair, which you can use with a younger baby.

- Clip-on seat. This clips on to your own table and is for babies who can sit up properly. The advantage is that your baby can sit up with the rest of the family at mealtimes. It can be useful to have if you are out visiting but you need to be sitting with your baby at all times as the clip-on mechanism can work loose. You can also only use them on sturdy tables, as when you put your baby in the seat his weight can tip the table over.

### SECONDHAND GOODS

Buying baby equipment is expensive and it can be tempting to buy cheaply from small ads or car boot sales. You may also feel that you are conserving natural resources by reusing equipment. But safety experts warn that in the UK around 15,000 children under the age of five are injured each year in home accidents involving nursery equipment.

Hidden dangers include:

- no instructions

- worn fittings and harnesses

- hairline cracks

- designs that no longer conform to current safety standards.

In the UK there is pressure to tighten the legislation governing the sale of secondhand nursery goods. You need to consider whether a secondhand product under stress will really protect your child and how you are going to assemble a highchair or cot with no instructions to help you. You also have no way of knowing if the previous owners have used it properly and there is no guarantee should anything go wrong.

Common problems with secondhand purchases are:

- worn bearings on pushchairs which cause wheel wobble.

- brakes that have become worn and less efficient.

- car seats need to be fitted correctly to be effective. If there is an accident your seat will not protect your baby unless it is properly fitted.

- once a car seat has been in an accident, it will have incurred damage or stress and is no longer safe to use.

- a secondhand cot may be missing essential components to hold it together and it could collapse.

- when you buy wooden items secondhand, the wood may be cracked or split and the paint used may contain lead or other substances that could harm your baby.

- using a secondhand cot mattress that is too small for your child's cot could lead to him being suffocated in the gap around the edge.

- a stair gate (see Safety at home on page 155) needs to be fitted properly to do its job correctly, otherwise it is not worth having. If it is second hand, it may prove difficult to fit

Clearly it is sensible to buy new products if at all possible. Choose carefully and avoid some of the unnecessary extra gadgets and gimmicks on the market, to save money. If you purchase a car seat that will take you through several years and children and a cot that will convert into a bed, for example, it is possible to make your money go much further.

### TIME OUT

Don't forget to allow your baby plenty of opportunity to lie fully stretched on the floor. Put down a blanket or activity mat and a few toys and let him roll, kick and try to push himself up. This will strengthen his muscles and help him to develop the necessary skills for sitting and crawling. Some doctors are concerned that babies who spend too much time restricted in seats do not get a chance to learn these essential skills.

# Safety at home

Babies are programmed to explore. From the moment of birth, your baby will start learning to co-ordinate his reflexes to make himself mobile. First he will manage to lift his head, then he will start to reach out and grab at whatever looks interesting. Next he will surprise you by rolling right over when you change his nappy.

Once he has learned to crawl you will be amazed at how much ground he covers in just a few seconds. Then, sometime around his first birthday, he will manage to pull himself up and 'cruise' around the furniture. Your helpless baby is now a highly mobile toddler and, for the next few years, you will have to watch his every move to protect him from the many hidden dangers lurking in your home.

Accidents are now the major cause of death for children under five. Every year in the UK, around 600,000 of them have to be admitted to hospital because of injuries caused by an accident in the home, so it's vital to take proper safety precautions.

## IN THE KITCHEN

- Move all household cleaners and bleaches from the cupboard under the sink to a locked cupboard high up on the wall. You could reduce the amount of dangerous chemicals in your home by using bicarbonate of soda to clean sinks, fridge, plastic tops and cooker top. Use salt and boiling water to keep the drains clean and half a cupful of vinegar added to a bucket of water to clean cork, tiled or lino floors.

- Buy safety locks and attach them to kitchen cupboards and drawers.

- Use the back rings on your cooker and turn pan handles inwards. A cooker guard gives added protection.

- Push the kettle to the back of the worktop and check the flex is well out of reach. Water in the kettle remains scalding hot long after it has boiled. Unplug the kettle, toaster and other electrical appliances when they are not in use so your child cannot turn them on accidentally.

- Put tablecloths away for a couple of years. A crawling baby can pull a cloth and the table contents on to his head.

- Keep plates, knives, cups of coffee and tea in the centre of the table.

- Make sure your baby is strapped into his high chair before you dish up hot food to the rest of the family.

- If your kitchen is very small, fit a safety gate to the entrance so your child cannot get in while you are cooking.

- Wrap up any sharp objects before you put them in the rubbish bin.

- Fit safety locks to the fridge and freezer.

### IN THE SITTING ROOM

- Fit safety covers to all plug sockets so your baby cannot push his fingers or toys into the holes.

- Keep a fireguard in front of a gas or open fire fixed to the wall. You will still need to keep your baby away

from it, as the guard itself can become very hot. Don't use a loose-standing guard, as it will be easy to pull over.

- Fix a film of safety glass to patio doors. You could also put coloured stickers on the glass so your baby realises it is solid.

- Move your video and TV out of reach.

- Remove any precious ornaments and household plants that may be poisonous.

- Fit plastic safety corners to sharp-edged table tops.

- Pin permanent flexes to the skirting board.

- Never place a mirror above a fire or radiator.

- Keep your baby's toys in a box at floor level so that he can reach them safely.

- Move cupboards or units that could tip over if he tries to pull himself up on them.

### IN THE BATHROOM

- Keep all toiletries, cosmetics and medicines in a locked bathroom cabinet.

- Use a non-slip bath mat for your baby's bath.

- Always run the cold tap before the hot

### KEEPING YOUR BABY SAFE

- You may consider buying a playpen. It should have a built-in floor, so your baby cannot move it around. Traditional models are square and made from wood, although you can buy mesh-sided ones to. A playpen may be useful if you have a spacious kitchen or sitting room and want to keep your baby safe while you are busy. Don't leave your baby in the playpen for long periods of time and make sure he can see you and has toys to play with. If you decide to use a playpen, introduce it to him before he can move about so that he can get use to it as a nice place to be in, rather than a curtailment of his fun.

- A safety gate will stop your child from climbing the stairs or entering a room. Make sure it fits properly and can be operated by an adult but not by a child. The safest models can be fixed to the wall. This may mark your wallpaper but the peace of mind is worth it. Don't buy a model that you need to climb over – your baby will soon start trying to copy you.

- A pram net is useful to place over the pram or carrycot if there are cats around. This will prevent them from curling up on top of your baby. It will also protect your baby against insects.

one and check the water temperature with your elbow before putting your baby in the bath.

- If you are using a baby bath you may find it safer to place it on the floor, rather than on a surface from which your baby could slip and fall.

- Check your hot tap does not leak and bath your baby with his head well away from the taps. Tie a towel or dishcloth round the hot tap if you are concerned that it may scald him.

- Never leave any child under five unattended in the bathroom. They can drown in just a few centimetres of water.

### IN THE NURSERY

- Ensure that all mobiles are hanging where your baby cannot reach and pull them down.

- Keep your nappy changing equipment and toiletries, including nappy sacks, well away from the side of the cot, so your baby

cannot reach out and grab them. Never leave plastic bags in your baby's room.

- Buy flame-proofed nightwear for

### GENERAL SAFETY RULES

- Check any equipment you buy for the symbol guaranteeing that it conforms to latest safety standards. In the UK the kitemark and a number indicates that an item conforms to the current British standard.

- Move all furniture away from windows.

- Fit a smoke alarm in your house and check the battery every six months by holding a candle just snuffed out near to it.

- Never carry or pass cups of coffee or tea or pans of boiling or hot water above your child's head.

- Never tie a dummy round your baby's neck – the ribbon could strangle him.

toddlers. Avoid dressing girls in long nighties once they are mobile, as they are likely to trip and fall. Nighties are also dangerous because they may become caught in the bars of a gas or electric fire.

- Don't use open-weave blankets that could trap little fingers.

- Never use a duvet or pillow with a baby under one year old, because of the risk of suffocation.

- Think hard before you buy a cot bumper. The ends must be cut short and tied securely to prevent them from coming undone and getting caught round your baby's neck or wrapped tightly round a finger.

- Never put your baby in his cot wearing a bib. Avoid any clothes with ribbons or cords that could pull tight round the neck.

- Change your baby on the floor to avoid the risk of him rolling off his changing mat.

## THE HALL AND STAIRS

- Fit safety gates to the top and bottom of the stairs (see below) to prevent your child from climbing up or falling down.

- Be careful when you answer the front door. Never leave it open – your baby can crawl out in a matter of seconds.

- Avoid polished floors and loose rugs that your child could slip on.

- Make sure the telephone and telephone table are in a safe place.

- Always hold on to the bannisters when you carry your baby up and downstairs.

- Check that your baby isn't able to get his head stuck between the bannisters.

### Baby walkers

Safety organisations have been campaigning for these to be banned. A walker is designed to allow your child to move around in an upright position before he has learnt to walk. Tragedies have occurred when babies have tipped themselves into fires and down the stairs. Additionally, experts say that babies left in them for long periods don't get the chance to practise walking properly, delaying their development.

# Toys and play

Babies have an enormous amount to learn and their natural curiosity, combined with proper stimulation and encouragement from you, will ensure that they quickly start to discover how the world works.

### Stimulation

As well as learning to control his own body and explore the world about him, your baby needs stimulation for another important reason. During his first three years, his brain will grow faster than at any other time. At birth his brain will weigh just 350 g, but by the age of three it will have grown to 1.35 kg. At the same time, important connections are developing between the

### Safety first

- Choose a toy that has a kitemark indicating it conforms to British safety standards. The CE mark is used on toys to indicate they meet European safety standards. The Lionmark is an indication of both quality and safety.

- In Britain only about 5% of toys do not conform to safety standards. Dangerous stuffing, sharp edges, eyes on wires or spikes, small parts that may come unattached and cause choking are all potentially lethal to small children. Do not buy a secondhand toy or toys from a market stall unless you can see an approved safety stamp.

different brain cells. A baby who does not receive adequate stimulation may have difficulty making those connections, giving him a poor start to life.

### The most important toy

Toy manufacturers are keen to promote a whole range of baby toys which claim to be educational and provide learning opportunities, and it is true that a few well-chosen toys can help your baby to explore the world about him. But you are his most important toy. If you smile and talk to him, carry him around so he is part of the family and can watch you during your daily routine, if you respond quickly to his needs, give him lots of cuddles, take him out and about and point out what's going on, play peek-a-boo and hand-clapping games, he will thrive.

### Choosing toys

Before you buy your baby toys, consider these points:

- Try to see the toy from your baby's point of view. You may find a cuddly teddy appealing but he would much prefer something designed for little hands to hold and manoeuvre.

- Although many baby toys are made in pastel colours, young babies find strong colours much more attractive.

- For the first year or so, your baby may prefer playing with the paper that his toys were wrapped in. He will also not know the difference between an expensive toy and a pile of empty plastic ice-cream cartons. Once he can sit up in the bath, give him a set of plastic beakers and smooth-edged empty yoghurt cartons to play with.

- Older babies may feel overwhelmed by too many bright, plastic toys. Choose natural wooden ones, too, to get him used to more subtle colours.

- Remember that everything is new and interesting to a baby. Leaves waving in the breeze, rain, birds, flowers are all fascinating – and free. Make sure he has the chance to look at the natural world around him and that you spare the time to point it out and talk about it.

### AGE GUIDELINES

Many manufacturers try to give guidelines to the age range each toy is suitable for. Use these if you are not sure whether one is right for your baby but don't be disappointed if he can't perform all the activities or if he doesn't show interest in it. Each baby is an individual who will develop at a different rate. One baby may be quick to learn to pull levers and buttons, while another may enjoy looking in detail at pictures and exploring the texture of a soft toy. Here are some tried and tested toys:

*From birth*
- Playmat. This consists of a variety of activities and fabrics. Your baby will enjoy lying on it for short periods of time

### HOMEMADE TOYS

- Mobile. String together pieces of silver foil and coloured card. Dry pasta pieces will rattle together to make an interesting noise. Hang this in the room where your baby sleeps. Secure it safely well out of his reach.

- Rattle. Use a small plastic bottle filled with lentils. Make sure the top is securely fastened.

- Large cardboard box. An older baby will love crawling into and out of a box.

- Give your baby a wooden spoon and a collection of pots and pans from the kitchen. Let him bang the pots to make different sounds.

- Peek-a-boo. At about ten months your baby will start to enjoy games where you 'hide' a toy or a beaker, covering it with a cloth, so he has to crawl to find it.

long before he learns how to ring the bells and move the squeakers.

- Rattle. Choose a soft rattle for a young baby. As he learns to manipulate it he is bound to catch himself with it and a hard plastic rattle could hurt.

- Baby gym. Your baby can lie underneath this and try to catch the balls and toys suspended above him. Colourful pictures at his eye level will provide something bright to focus on.

*From three months*
- Activity centre. This attaches to the side of your baby's cot. It has a range of mirrors, balls, squeakers and rattles that he can learn to manipulate.

- Soft ball, bricks. He will enjoy exploring the texture of these long before he can throw or stack them.

*From six months*
- Shape sorter. Your baby will enjoy pushing shapes through different-sized holes. He will also like to shake the sorter when it is full.

- Cloth or board books. This is the perfect time to introduce your baby to books. Choose ones with familiar themes that your baby will recognise – cats and dogs not dinosaurs or dragons. Buy one or two bath books for bathtime.

- Stacking rings, bricks, beakers. Your baby will enjoy knocking down the towers you build him long before he manages to construct one himself. He can also explore the different sizes and colours.

*From one year*
- Push-along toy. As your baby gets near to taking his first steps, a push-along trolley

### Toy libraries

In the UK there are several hundred toy lending libraries. You can borrow safe toys in good condition for your baby to try out for a few weeks. The staff are often pleased to give advice on which toys are suitable.

or truck will encourage him. He will also enjoy putting his bricks and beakers inside it.

*From 18 months*
- A sit-and-ride toy will encourage co-ordination. Make sure he does not ride it near hazards.

- Simple lift-out puzzles with large, easy-to-handle pieces will develop his matching and concentration skills. Help him at first.

# Your baby's development

During his first year your baby will develop the following important skills:

- Language. He will learn to understand words long before he can speak. By about eight months he may be making noises that sound like 'dadada' or 'mamama'. By his first birthday, you should hear his first word and he will acquire two or three new words each month. The 'd' sound is the easiest to say, so it sounds as if your baby is saying daddy before mummy. It's nothing personal! Psychologists have noticed that a baby's language skills develop more quickly if adults speak to him using proper words and sentences, rather than baby language.

- Movement. During his first six months, he will learn to roll over and sit up. During his second six months, his co-ordination and muscle control will enable him to sit, crawl (eight months), bottom shuffle or 'cruise' (ten months) around the furniture. Sometime between his first birthday and 18 months, your child will walk with confidence.

- Listening. His listening skills will become more finely attuned. By 12–16 weeks he will be able to locate where a sound is coming from and will look to see it. Between six and eight months he will respond to his own name.

- Hand-eye co-ordination. From five months, he will learn to use his hands and eyes together so that if he sees an object he will be able to reach out and grasp it.

- Hand control. At first your baby will use his whole hand to pick something up. Then from eight months he will learn to use the palm of his hand and his fingers together – this is known as the palmar grip. Finally, by 15 months, he will mange to pick up small objects with just his thumb and first finger – this is known as the pincer grip.

- Two-handed play. From seven months he will learn to pass an object from one hand to the other.

- Visual tracking. At four weeks he recognises his mother's face. At 12–20 weeks he knows when things are familiar and looks at his hands. At 20–28 weeks, he can see 800 times better than he did at birth. By nine and ten months your baby will be able to follow a rapidly moving object – his vision will be almost as good as yours.

- Object permanence. At about seven months your baby will realise that if an object or person disappears from view they still exist. He will therefore look for a toy if he drops it, for example. This often coincides with the begining of a clingy phase which peaks at around nine months, when he is anxious that you may not return once you leave his sight.

- Learn to remember. In the early weeks of life babies act on reflexes. By two months they start to replace these with voluntary actions. Until three months they can only do one voluntary action at a time – reach for a rattle but not cry at the same time. By the time they are six months old, babies can do two things at once.

### HOW YOUR BABY GROWS

- Weight. This will have trebled by 12–14 months.

- Height. He will have grown by 25–30 cm by his first birthday.

- Teeth. These start to appear from five to six months.

# CHAPTER SIX

# Outdoor Life

From the time your baby is a couple of weeks old, you will start to go out and about with him. From about three months, he will enjoy looking around at the shapes and colours – trees waving in the breeze above him, cars rushing past, dogs and cats, people and flowers. And as he develops, you will find yourself looking at the world through new eyes when you see how ordinary, everyday objects look special to your baby.

### TIME FOR A WALK

Going for a walk is not only important for your baby but for you as well, as you will both benefit from the fresh air and exercise. Aim to get out twice a day whether it is just a quick visit to the park or a stroll to the shops. Looking at the same four walls is as monotonous for him as it is for you. Even when you are pegging out washing, wrap him up and take him outside in his seat or pushchair for a change of scene.

# In the garden

Your baby will love spending time in the garden and it will offer fun and adventure to a growing child, whatever the size.

### SAFETY OUTSIDE

Once your baby starts to crawl you will need to be as vigilant about safety outdoors as you are inside the home. Garden tools and machinery can all cause serious injury if left around or in an unlocked shed. At this stage, your baby will be putting anything he comes across in his mouth – and that may include poisonous plants and small stones.

Keep your child safe in the garden:

- Never let him play in it unattended.

- Don't let him pick up earth – it may be contaminated with chemicals or animal droppings.

- Make sure that gates are locked and all fences are secure.

- If you have a garden pond fence it off - or, better still, fill it in. Empty your

paddling pool immediately after use and never leave your baby or toddler in it unsupervised. Drowning is one of the

### DANGER

- Vomiting and abdominal pain are signs of food poisoning. If you think your child has eaten a poisonous plant, take him to hospital at once with a sample of the plant you suspect he has eaten.

- If your child swallows any garden chemicals take him to hospital immediately with the container holding the chemical. Do not try to make him sick. If his lips or mouth show signs of burning, cool them by giving water or milk to drink.

- Some poisons work on the central nervous system preventing breathing so if he is unconscious, try to keep his airway open by tilting his head backwards and pushing his chin up to lift his tongue clear.

most common accidents in the home with under fives.

- Keep all garden chemicals on a high shelf in a locked room or shed.

- Cover your baby's pram with a safety net. As well as keeping cats off him, this will also catch any leaves or debris that may get blown up on a breezy day.

- Never start your car without knowing exactly where your toddler is.

- Put any play equipment on grass, not a hard surface.

- Teach your child not to eat berries.

- Pull up any poisonous plants. These include deadly nightshade, death cap fungus, laburnum and foxglove.

### DOGS

If you have a dog he should be trained to reduce the risk of him biting. A normally docile animal can become frustrated if he is continually mauled by a baby or toddler and may snap in irritation. Occasionally dogs have been known to turn on small

### FIRST AID KIT

Keep your first aid equipment in a clean, dry container where you can eaily find it. Keep a kit in the car, too, and take antiseptic wipes on outings to clean cuts and grazes.

You will need:
- non-stick sterile wound dressings
- triangular bandage to make a sling or secure a dressing
- crepe bandage to hold dressings in place
- cotton wool
- calamine lotion or camomile cream to soothe insect bites, stings and sunburn
- assorted plasters
- scissors, tweezers and safety pins
- anti-histamine cream for stings
- tube of antiseptic cream
- arnica cream for bruises
- calendula cream (marigold) for cuts
- eucalyptus oil – insect repellant

children causing serious injury. Encourage your baby to be interested in animals and to treat them with respect, kindness – and caution. Don't let him treat them like toys.

Be especially wary of dogs like German shepherds, Doberman pinschers and bull terriers, which have been bred for guarding purposes. Teach your baby not to touch them or go near them but try not to instil fear in him so that he panics whenever he sees one.

Children are at risk from catching toxocara, a form of roundworm, from dog excrement. Children touching this may get the eggs on their fingers and swallow them.

### DANGER

Rabies is a potentially fatal condition spread by the saliva of infected animals. Although it is not found in the UK it is endemic in many other countries. If you are abroad and your baby is bitten by an animal that may have rabies, he will need a course of injections urgently and must be taken straight to hospital.

Once in the gut the eggs hatch and the larvae migrate to the eyes, causing blindness, or to the lungs, causing wheezing and fever.

If you have a dog, clean up your own garden and worm him regularly. You should also scoop up dog's mess when you take him out for a walk.

### CATS

Toxoplasmosis is an infection that can be acquired from handling cat faeces (or eating undercooked meat or unwashed salad). It may cause a mild infection or illness similar to glandular fever – sore throat, tiredness and enlarged glands. Pregnant women, however, are at much more serious risk. Miscarriage, stillbirth, hydrocephalus, jaundice and eye disorders may result. If you are pregnant do not change a cat litter tray. Keep cat litter trays out of reach of toddlers and make sure that you wash your hands before eating. Worm your cat every three months. Keep cats and dogs away from work surfaces and give them separate food and drink bowls. More information is available from the Toxoplasmosis Trust (see Useful Addresses).

### ANIMAL BITES

Animals have sharp, pointed teeth that leave deep puncture wounds, injecting the germs they harbour in their mouths deep into the tissues. If your baby or child is bitten:

- stay calm. Bites are rarely serious but if left untreated they can become infected.

- wash the wound thoroughly with soapy water for five minutes to remove any blood, saliva or dirt. Apply antiseptic cream and cover it with a clean dressing.

- take your baby to the doctor to have the wound checked. If it is deep it may carry the risk of tetanus or becoming infected. Your baby should be protected against tetanus once he has had his first two jabs (at two and three months).

- press firmly on a serious wound with a clean cloth to stem the flow of bleeding. Then cover it with a dressing and take your baby straight to hospital.

### INSECT BITES AND STINGS

Your baby is most likely to be stung or bitten by bees, hornets or ants, or parasites, like fleas, or mosquitoes. Insects breed most rapidly during hot, damp weather. If your baby is crawling, put him in long trousers, so his legs are not in direct contact with the grass. Place a groundsheet over the grass for him to sit and play on. Once he is walking keep him away from flower beds where bees gather and don't give him fruit juice or sweet things which attract wasps.

*What you can do*

- Like animal bites, insect bites and stings should be cleaned with warm water and soap. Try to avoid soap containing detergent, perfume or other irritants (see Baby toiletries on pages 63–8)

- After cleaning, rinse the wound in clean water and apply antiseptic cream.

*Flea and mosquito bites*
- Keep dogs and cats free of fleas and encourage them to sleep only in a special basket.

- Treat bites with calamine or antihistamine cream. Badly bitten children should see a doctor.

*Ant bites*
- Do not let your baby sit on uncovered grass.

- Treat bites with bicarbonate of soda paste (two teaspoons of bicarbonate of soda mixed with a little water).

*Nettle stings*
- Pull out any patches of nettles in your garden.

- The sting is acid, so bicarbonate of soda mixed with a little water into a paste will ease the pain. Use cool leaves or water in an emergency.

- Treat long-lasting irritation with calamine lotion.

*Bee stings*
- These are one of the most dangerous stings a child can receive in Britain or other temperate climate because of a risk of heart failure associated with anaphylactic shock. This severe reaction is characterised by nettlerash, dizzines, facial and throat swelling, wheeziness, breathing difficulties, vomiting and collapse. Urgent medical attention is required – a shot of adrenaline is given followed by a course of injections to stop it from happening again.

- You can often see the black sting sticking out of the centre of a white area of skin which is surrounded by a swollen red bump.

- Scrape the sting away from the base with a knife blade or clean fingernail or remove it with tweezers, grasping the sting below the venom sac and taking

### COLD COMPRESS

There are two types of cold compress you can make:

- Soak a pad of cotton wool or towelling in cold or iced water. Squeeze it out so that it is wet but not dripping and place it on the injury.

- Replace or drip more water on to the pad after a few minutes. Continue cooling the area for 30 minutes.

- If necessary, keep the compress in place with a bandage.

- Fill a plastic bag half-full with crushed ice. Add a little salt to lower the melting temperature.

- Seal the bag and wrap it in a cloth.

- Place it on the injury and continue cooling for 30 minutes.

- If necessary hold the pack in place with a bandage.

care not to squeeze the sac of poison which will only release more venom.

- Treat the area with bicarbonate of soda paste as for ant bites (above), or use surgical spirit or a cold compress (see box).

- If there is an allergic reaction severe swelling will occur very fast. Apply a cold compress while you take your child straight to hospital.

- Stings in the mouth may cause swelling which obstructs breathing. Give your child a mouthwash of one teaspoon of bicarbonate of soda to a tumbler of water, followed by crushed ice to suck. Take him straight to hospital with the dead bee if you can find it.

- Multiple bee stings require urgent medical attention.

*Wasp stings*
- These sometimes cause an allergic reaction, with severe swelling or shock similar to a bee sting.

- The puncture may contain a black sting.

Take it out carefully with tweezers, a sterilised needle or clean fingernails.

- Don't squeeze as you might push the poison further into the skin.

- The surrounding area will be white, then reddened and swollen as with a bee sting.

- Wasp stings contain alkali venom. After cleansing, dress the wound with vinegar or lemon juice as the acid will help to neutralise the venom. Use an antihistamine cream if you haven't got any. Avoid rubbing the skin.

- If there is a lot of swelling use a cold compress (see page 168). Treat stings in the mouth as for bee stings (see page 167).

- Multiple wasp stings require urgent medical attention.

### SNAKE BITES

In Europe the viper or adder is the snake most likely to bite. It has a broad head and black zig-zag markings on its back. About 75 cm long, it may be grey, yellow or reddish brown. If your child is bitten:

- keep calm and reassure him. Fear can cause shock.

- wash the bite with soap and water and remove any venom you can see.

- cover the wound with a clean dressing and get medical help.

- sweating, vomiting and diarrhoea are all rare reactions but be on the look out for them.

- when you are abroad, seek medical attention urgently. Try to remember what the snake looked like.

### SHOCK

Shock can result from a bite or sting if there is severe allergy, pain or stress. Watch out for symptoms such as pale skin, restlessness, confusion, anxiety, quickened pulse and rapid breathing.

*What you can do*
- Lay your child on his side and, if he is wounded, try to stem any bleeding by pressing on the wound with a clean pad (see page 170).

- Loosen clothing and cover the child with a light blanket.

- Don't offer a drink.

- Get medical help immediately.

### HEAVY BLEEDING

If blood spurts from a wound or flows for longer than a couple of minutes, you need to stem it so that the blood can clot.

*What you can do*

- Raise the injured part to reduce the amount of blood flowing to it.

- Place a pad of clean cloth, such as a tea towel, over the wound. Press hard on it for 10 minutes. Or press with your fingers, drawing the edges of the cut firmly together.

- Bind the pad in place with a bandage. If the blood soaks through, place another pad over the top and maintain pressure.

- If something is embedded in the wound, raise the injured part, apply pressure around the object, not directly on it as this will push it further in. Don't try to pull the object out or to clean the wound.

- Release the pressure for a moment and roll up a small piece of material into a sausage. Then twist into a ring.

- Place the ring around the embedded object, cover with gauze and bandage it in place. Don't bandage tightly over the wound.

# Life-saving techniques

Memorise this section carefully so you can act quickly in an emergency. Every second counts. If your baby or child stops breathing you can breathe your own air into his lungs to prevent brain damage. Don't give up – children have revived after several hours of being unconscious.

### ARTIFICIAL RESPIRATION

If your baby or child is unconscious and has stopped breathing you need to start artificial respiration right away.

*For a baby*

- Slide one hand under your baby's neck and tilt his head back, but not too far. Leave your other hand on his forehead.

- Take a breath, then place your lips around the baby's mouth and nose and breathe out gently.

- Watch your baby's chest to see whether it rises as you breathe out.

- If his chest does not rise you will need to unblock his windpipe (see Choking, see opposite).

- Give four more breaths into the baby's nose and mouth then feel his pulse at the side of his neck – not his wrist – to see if his heart is beating.

- If his heart is beating, continue breathing into your baby's lungs, at the rate of one breath every three seconds, until he starts to breathe on his own or emergency help arrives.

- As soon as he starts to breathe unaided, turn him on his side into the recovery position (see page 172).

*For a child*

- Follow the above procedure but seal your mouth over his mouth only and pinch his nostrils to prevent air from escaping.

### CHOKING

Your baby will constantly be putting things in his mouth, so you need to be vigilant at all times, taking anything small out of his reach. However, if your child or baby is struggling for breath, is not making any noise and is going blue around the mouth, you must take immediate action.

*For a baby*

- Hold him face down and strike him between the shoulder blades four times. (See diagram A overleaf.)

- If he is still choking lay him on his side and tilt his head back.

- Support his back with one hand, and place two fingers of your other hand halfway between his navel and the bottom of his ribs. (See diagram B.)

- Press inwards and upwards with a sharp,

**A**

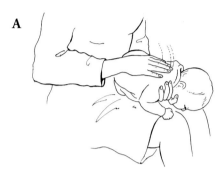

**B**

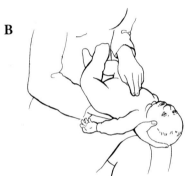

thrusting movement to dislodge the blockage.

*For a child*

- Sit or kneel and lay your child over your knee, with his head hanging down.

- Support his chest with one hand and strike him several times between the shoulder blades.

- If the blockage remains, sweep round your child's mouth with a finger and try to dislodge it from the back of his throat.

- Sit him on your lap, facing forwards, and press sharply inwards and upwards four times halfway between his navel and the

### RECOVERY POSITION

Put your baby or child in the recovery position if he is breathing but unconscious:

- Lie him on his front with his head turned to one side and his chin jutting forwards to stop his tongue from blocking the airway.

- Bend his top arm and leg at right angles for extra support.

- Cover him with a coat or blanket and check his breathing every three minutes.

*Danger*
Do not move your baby or child if you think he may have a spine injury.

bottom of his ribs. Tuck your thumb in and make a fist to do this.

### If his heart stops

If your baby or child's heart stops, you must pump it manually to keep blood circulating round his body. To do this:

- Slide one hand under your child's shoulders and grasp the top of his arm.

- With your other hand find the bottom of his breast bone, then measure halfway up to his neck.

- Place two fingers for a baby, or the heel of your hand for a child, just below the middle of his breastbone and press down around 2 cm.

- Release the pressure.

- Repeat at a rate of two per second five times. Then breathe into his lungs. Continue with five compressions followed by one breath until help arrives.

- When his heart starts beating again, stop giving compressions but continue with artificial respiration.

# Street wise

After the home, most accidents that happen to children occur in the street. Even a baby in a pushchair can be at risk, as he will stick out in front of you by about a metre. So be careful not to push him into the road while you are waiting to cross.

Remember not to hang heavy bags over the pushchair handles, as it can easily overbalance. When you stop always put on the brake and never leave a child unattended or a dog tied to your baby's pram or pushchair.

If you also have an older child you need to hold his hand while you are walking along the pavement, until you can trust him to keep hold of the side of the pram. You could invest in a pair of safety reins, although some toddlers hate wearing these. Or it might be safer to put both children in a double buggy when you are taking them out in streets with heavy traffic.

### Crossing safely

Teach your child how to cross the road as soon as it's possible. Each time you cross, explain to him what you are doing so that it becomes automatic.

- Find a safe place to cross, such as a pedestrian crossing, traffic lights or, in the country, a straight piece of road with no traffic visible in either direction.

- Stop at the kerb, look right, left, then right again and listen for traffic.

- If traffic is coming, let it pass.

- Look right, left, then right again and if the road is clear, walk – don't run – across it.

- Warn your child never to chase a ball into the street or to stand or play behind parked cars.

### STRANGER DANGER

From an early age you need to talk to your child about keeping safe. Sadly paedophiles may seem perfectly respectable and around two-thirds of them are not strangers, but adults already known to the child. Paedophiles are good at making friends with children and hang around playgrounds and parks where children are likely to be. Some find their victims through babysitting and babies, who cannot tell what has been going on, are particularly at risk. On the other hand, there are plenty of elderly people who love talking to babies and are completely harmless. But never leave your child alone with anyone who offers to care for him, while you pop into a shop, for example.

To protect your child:

- check on anyone who is left in charge of your child. Talk, as well as write, to other people they have worked for.

- explain to children the difference between safe and unsafe secrets. A secret about a birthday surprise is fine, but no one should ever ask them to keep kisses or touches secret.

- never send anyone to collect your child from a childminder or playgroup without warning the adult in charge and, once he is old enough to understand, warn the child himself.

- When he is older, arrange to have a

family codeword. Tell him that if anyone else comes to collect him, he or she will always know the codeword. 'No code, no go.'

- most paedophiles are not strangers. Your child must know that if anyone touches him in a confusing or frightening way he must tell you.

- tell him to make a loud fuss. If someone tries to touch or grab him he should shout 'No', run away and tell an adult. Practise 'Yell, run, tell'.

- For more information contact Kidscape in Useful Addresses, page 188–189.

### Choosing a babysitter

It's important that you and your partner enjoy time together away from the responsibilities of caring for your baby. To do that you need to choose a reliable babysitter.

- Find someone through personal recommendation if possible. If you are new to an area ask your health visitor if she knows of a good babysitter or join a local babysitting circle.

- Don't employ anyone under 16. If you do use a teenager check that she has access to an adult.

### Playground safety

One of the favourite outings for an older baby or toddler is a trip to the park or playground. Once your baby can sit upright you can put him in one of the boxed-in baby swings and push him gently to and fro. Playgrounds usually have special areas for babies and toddlers. Keep to these, as older children play more boisterously. Watch out for children running behind the swings.

If there is a baby slide he will enjoy going down this, with you holding him firmly at all times. Check that the slide is one continuous piece with no jointed panels and that the surface beneath it is specially designed to cushion any falls.

- Ask the babysitter to come to your house before your evening out so you can see how well she gets on with your child.

- Ask how much experience she has had and get names and addresses of other families she has worked for so you can contact them.

- Ask if she knows any first aid.

- Ask what she would do in an emergency.

- Explain how much you will pay.

- Explain how you want her to deal with any problems – for example, if your baby won't settle or wakes during the evening.

- On the actual evening, make sure you leave a number where you can be contacted and the number of your local hospital and GP.

- Trust your instincts. If you are not happy, use someone else.

# Chemical sprays

Officials now admit that, in the UK, there are traces of chemicals from sprays in all our food, including bread, fruit and breastmilk, as well as in our bodies, the soil, water and atmosphere (see Feeding Your Baby pages 37–9). But they claim that the amounts are too small to do any damage. This is the result of the farming industry's adoption of chemical spraying techniques to improve crop yields.

### PESTICIDES

- Pesticides, which get rid of the insects that eat and lay eggs in our food crops, have been linked to cancer, as well as allergies and birth defects.

- Many of the pesticides still used in Britain have been banned overseas. Some are related to nerve gases, poisons and drugs which suppress the immune system and the ability to fight disease.

- Under European law, the British Government has been required to set Maximum Residue Limits (MRLs) for pesticide residues on some fruit and vegetables. But some pesticides remain unregulated. Tecnazene, commonly used on potatoes, is one example. Campaigners link it to birth defects and cancers, although officials deny there is any health risk associated with it.

• Amounts of pesticide residue on fruit crops vary dramatically. A survey by the Pesticides Safety Directorate has shown that individual pieces of fruit can contain up to 30 times the average for the batch. Eating a single apple could take you over the acceptable level of intake.

• Some supermarkets have attempted to support schemes to reduce the use of pesticides by buying from suppliers who follow a system known as Integrated Crop Management (ICM). This system is intended to reduce the total number of pesticides used on each crop. But critics point out that, although the total number of chemicals used may be declining slightly, their levels of toxicity are increasing to compensate for this. And under ICM there are still 68

different pesticides permitted on potatoes and 56 on strawberries, to name just two examples.

• Environmental experts believe that if the supermarkets had to list the chemicals used on the crops next to their displays, consumers would be shocked into demanding stronger controls.

• In the 1950s in the US, around 35 per cent of harvest were lost to pests. Today 30 per cent is still lost but to different pests, and now the soil and our bodies contain the residue of around 12 persistent chemicals! Environmentalists are calling for tougher regulations to limit the use of these toxic chemicals so that consumers can be sure they food they buy for their children is safe to eat.

### FUNGICIDES

In 1990 in the US, fungicide manufacturers warned farmers to stop using their sprays on apples, beans, cabbage, berries, lettuces, melons, oats and strawberries after the American Environmental Protection

Agency threatened to ban them. This followed the revelation that they could cause up to 125,000 cases of cancer. Children are thought to be particularly at risk because they are physically small and so consume proportionately higher quantities of dangerous chemicals. There is also plenty of time in which the chemicals can trigger the onset of cancer in later life. British farmers have not received a similar warning.

Even washing and peeling fruit does not offer complete protection, because many chemicals penetrate right into the flesh.

Scientists are particularly concerned about ETU (thylene thiourea), a chemical that accumulates most in heat-treated foods such as tomato paste, ketchup and apple juice.

You can reduce the effect of chemicals on your child by:

- washing and peeling fruit.

- buying organic fruit and vegetables when you can afford to. These should still be washed but you can leave the fruit unpeeled, so your child can enjoy the valuable nutrients, which are lost when you have to discard the peel.

- buying bottled water. At least 16 toxic pesticides are commonly found in drinking water.

- avoiding walking in the countryside when farmers are spraying crops.

- joining one of the organisations campaigning for the closer supervision of pesticides (see Useful Addresses on pages 188–89).

### STRAWBERRY SURPRISE

Over the last 10 years strawberry growing in the UK has become much more intensive, partly due to the pesticide methyl bromide. Also used in the US to treat the soil before planting, it helps to produce firm-skinned, bright red strawberries. However, it is very damaging to the ozone layer (see Fun in the sun on pages 181–82). Although it doesn't leave harmful residues on the fruit, methyl bromide is a highly toxic chemical. Its use has been phased out in the Netherlands because of concern over water contamination. Many

European countries don't use it.

Methyl bromide is also used in the production of lettuces, celery, tomatoes, cucumbers and mushrooms. In addition it is used to fumigate soil, grains, nuts and herbs, as well as containers, machinery and processing facilities. Concern is so great that the developed countries have agreed that the use of this chemical should be phased out by 2010. Environmental experts argue that more urgent action needs to be taken.

*What you can do*

- Ask your supermarket or greengrocer for strawberries produced without methyl bromide.

- Find out whether your local pick-your-own strawberry fields use methyl bromide.

- Join an organisation campaigning against it (see Food Commission, page 188).

# Happy holidays

Holidays with babies and small children can be great fun but not necessarily relaxing. To have a successful holiday with a baby or toddler, you will need to accept that the limitations and extra work a baby brings do not disappear just because you have moved to a different part of the country or the world for a week or two.

### BOOKING YOUR HOLIDAY

Before you book, make sure that the destinations you are considering are truly baby-friendly. If the brochure does not provide enough detail, ask your travel agent to find out the following:

- Is it possible to guarantee a ground floor apartment or room? Anything above that level poses a risk if your child wanders out on to the balcony or staircase.

- Is there a nearby supply of nappies, baby toiletries and baby formula milk, or baby foods?

- Are cots and highchairs provided?

- Is there a baby listening or babysitting service? How often will the baby listener tune into your baby or, if you prefer to use the babysitting service, who will be doing the babysitting? Some hotels offer qualified nursery nurses, others rely on hotel staff.

- Are there any long flights of steps or steep hills?

- Will your room be well away from the nightlife, so your baby will not be disturbed?

- Will your room be safely away from the swimming pool and main road?

- Is there a washing machine available?

- Is there somewhere to dispose of used nappies?

- Will you be able to make up bottles of formula milk and baby meals safely?

TRAVELLING WITH A BABY

Whichever method of travel you take, build plenty of breaks into your journey, so you can feed and change your baby. Breastfeeding will be an asset. Once your baby is about four months old you might decide to holiday close to home until he is old enough to cope with longer journeys, as older babies and toddlers easily become restless and fractious. Some airline companies can provide a temporary cot for your baby to sleep in during a flight.

Make sure you take hand luggage or have a bag handy containing:

- nappies

- made-up bottles of formula milk

- jars of babyfood, spoons, bib

- spare set of clothes

- beaker of drink

- small toys for an older baby.

### SWIMMING POOLS

- Apart from drowning, swimming pools can pose another threat to small children if high levels of organochlorines are used to treat the water.

- Many pools use a salt treatment called sodium hypochlorite which is much safer, although sore eyes can result if organochlorines are also added. If you want to take your baby swimming find out how often the chlorine level is checked and what filter mechanisms are in place.

- Choose a pool that is regularly and well maintained.

- Young babies love swimming and many local pools run sessions especially for mothers and babies. But don't take your baby swimming until he has completed his first course of immunisations at four months (see Immunisation on page 102).

# Fun in the sun

It wasn't very long ago when parents were told that sunshine was good for their children and that a glowing tan was a sign of good health. To a great extent it still is – sunlight not only evokes a sense of well-being, it also promotes activity in the skin's cells which leaves people feeling full of energy. And vitamin D, present in sunlight, is essential for strong bones and teeth.

### COVER UP

Nowadays, we know that the sun's ultraviolet rays can cause great damage, especially to children:

- Sunburn increases the risk of skin cancer, which is now one of the fastest growing cancers in the UK with 40,000 new cases and 2,000 deaths each year, a dramatic 90 per cent increase in 25 years. Experts believe that today one bout of serious sunburn can put a child at risk of having skin cancer in later life.

- Malignant melanoma, the more dangerous form of skin cancer, is linked with exposure to short bursts of strong sunlight, such as annual two-week holidays exposed to the sun.

- The thinning of the ozone layer is making the problem worse, say the experts. Situated in the upper atmosphere, this layer of gases protects the earth by absorbing up to 99 per cent of the sun's damaging ultraviolet rays.

- The continued use of CFC gases (chlorofluorocarbons) in a wide variety of processes, including aerosol can sprays (see Household aids on page 136), is

having a devastating effect on the ozone layer. As it breaks down, it allows more of the harmful rays to reach the earth. However, the good news is that CFCs are no longer present in new fridges and household goods.

- In 1996 the ozone hole over the Antarctic measured twice the size of Europe. In the northern hemisphere the ozone layer has been depleted by up to 25 per cent, with substantial thinning over populated areas including Britain.

A HEALTHY TAN?

Children have thinner skin than adults so need more protection. Sunburn occurs when the small blood vessels under the skin dilate in an effort to protect it. The blood supply to the exposed area is increased, causing inflammation. The darker the skin the more melanin is present to protect it. Fair skins can't produce melanin quickly enough, so a lobster pink colour is the result. Fair skins that have been wrapped up all winter are the slowest to produce melanin. Red-headed children are most at risk.

*Protecting your baby*

- Keep a baby under six months out of strong sunlight. He can quickly overheat and dehydrate.

- In the summer, stay inside between 11 am and 3 pm when the rays are at their most intense. If you have to be out for part of that time make sure you are in the shade and that your children wear protective clothing (see page 185).

- Put toys in the shade. Remember that the sun moves round during the day so if you have a paddling pool you will need to change its position every couple of hours.

- Always use a parasol on your baby's pram or pushchair.

### RAYS OF SUNSHINE

The sun's rays can penetrate shade and haze and they can also be reflected off other surfaces. Less than half of them come from direct sunshine. The sun emits three types of rays:

- UVA rays reduce the elasticity of the skin and so help to cause premature ageing. They penetrate deeply, reaching the lower skin layers, causing the upper layers to thicken to protect them and eventually looking like leather.

- UVB rays cause freckling and sunburn.

They are absorbed by the skin's top layers and stimulate the production of vitamin D and a protective pigment called melanin which gives the skin its brown colour. UVB rays are most intense at midday, in hot climates and at high altitudes. These were thought to be more dangerous but scientists now say that both UVA and UVB rays can cause skin cancer (melanoma).

- UVC rays are the most damaging. These are the rays that the depleted ozone layer can no longer completely absorb.

- Gradually increase the amount of time your child spends in the sun. Don't let him stay out for longer than 20 minutes on the first day.

- The intensity of the sun's rays depend on where you are. Sand and sea, snow, high altitudes and windy weather all intensify the effects of the sun. UV rays pass through water and are reflected off snow.

### CHOOSING A SUNSCREEN

- Buy a sunscreen with a high sun protection factor from SPF15 to 30 for suncreams and SPF50 for blocks. The number indicates the extra protection the lotion gives against UVB rays above that provided by the child's own skin. So SPF15 means that if he wears this cream he can stay in the sun 15 times longer than he would be able to with no sunscreen lotion.

- Check the protection against UVA radiation. Most manufacturers use a star rating system to indicate how much protection is offered.

- Some high factor lotions can irritate a young child's skin, as they require higher concentrations of sunblocking chemicals. If in doubt stick to SPF 15 and re-apply every 30 minutes. Products containing benzophenones and para-aminobenzoic acid (PABA) are known for causing allergic skin rashes. Lanolin can cause a reaction, too.

- Sunscreens that contain zinc oxide and titanium dioxide, which are both natural chemicals, are the safest sunblocks to use on children.

- Some sunsreens leave a white film on the skin so you can see where you have applied it and check that no areas have been missed.

- Make sure you apply the sunscreen everywhere, including your child's feet, fingers, face, shoulders and the back of his neck. Pay particular attention to his nose and the tops of his ears.

- Re-apply it each time your child comes out of the water, even if the bottle claims it to be 'water-resistant'.

- After applying sunscreen wait 15–30 minutes for it to penetrate the skin before allowing your child into the sun.

- Store sunscreen creams and lotions out of the sun to prevent them from deteriorating.

TOO MUCH SUN

If your child has been in the sun for too long he may suffer the following reactions:

- Heat rash. Some babies and children develop a fine red rash in hot weather, either in or out of the sun. Treat this by

PROTECTIVE CLOTHING

- Shorts, long-sleeve T-shirts and cover-up swimwear in special fabrics offer extra protection. In the UK, sun-protective clothing is available from the Health Education Authority, as well as from larger retailers. Some clothes have a motif which changes colour as the temperature rises.

- Give him a cap with protective flaps at the sides and the back.

- Buy protective sunglasses. These are suitable for children from six months onwards. Make sure they conform to minimum safety standards (BS2724 in

the UK). Don't be tempted to buy cheap sunglasses. These may enable your child to see in bright sunlight without blinking but the sunlight will penetrate the lenses and burn the eyes behind the irises.

- If your child is wearing ordinary shorts and T-shirt remember that cotton offers less protection when it is damp, so you will still need to apply a sunscreen (see Choosing a sunscreen, page 184). Choose dark colours rather than light ones and avoid very stretchy material, which offers less protection.

taking your baby to a cooler room, bathing him in lukewarm water and patting his skin until almost dry. Let him sleep in just a vest and nappy so the rash is not irritated by clothes.

- Sunburn. Sometimes this is only evident a few hours after the damage has been done. Cool the skin by patting it with a cloth soaked in cool water. Use calamine lotion or a natural remedy such as aloe, marigold or myrrh to soothe the skin and reduce inflammation. Fresh cucumber juice and dock leaves also ease pain. Give infant paracetamol if he seems in pain.

If blisters develop you should take him to your accident and emergency department. Do not try to break them.

- Heat stroke. If your child develops a fever and seems unwell after being in the sun he may have heatstroke. Give him plenty to drink, wrap him in a cool, damp sheet and call the doctor or take him to a hospital.

*Danger*
Most cases of skin cancer are treatable if caught early enough. Freckles and moles are normal on children but you should consult your doctor if they change shape or colour, become inflamed or start to itch.

# In the countryside

Three million people currently belong to environmental and countryside groups in the UK. There are many practical ways of encouraging young children to take an interest in the countryside and outdoor life.

- Make your garden a pesticide-free zone. This will protect your child from chemical hazards and encourage local wildlife.

- Feed the birds in winter and provide nest boxes. Encourage your child to watch and recognise the different species of birds. Give them breadcrumbs, fruit, cheese and bacon scraps, cooked rice and oatmeal. Provide water for them to drink and bathe in, too.

- Leave a heap of logs and fallen leaves for hedgehogs to hibernate under.

- If you have a large enough garden, leave part of it to grow wild.

- Join the National Trust. It owns gardens, parks, downlands, lakes, mountains and coastline as well as historic buildings you can visit.

- If you live in a town or city, visit your nearest City Farm. There are 65 in the UK, running conservation and farming projects and teaching young children about looking after the countryside. (See Useful Addresses on page 188–89).

### IN THE YEARS AHEAD

As your baby grows older you can encourage him to take an interest in his environment and the issues surrounding it. Most of the organisations listed at the end of this book have junior memberships and run special activities for younger members.

By following some of the advice in this book, you will have not only brought up your baby to be happy and healthy, you

### FOLLOWING THE COUNTRY CODE

- Leave livestock, crops and machinery alone.
- Take your litter home.
- Help to keep all water clean.
- Protect wildlife, plants and trees.
- Take special care on country roads.
- Make no unnecessary noise.
- Enjoy the countryside and respect its life and work.
- Guard against all risk of fire.
- Fasten all gates.
- Keep your dog under close control.
- Keep to public paths across farmland.
- Use gates and stiles to cross fences, hedges and walls.

will also have helped to ensure that the next generation grows up to be even more concerned to protect and care for the world and its precious resources.

# Useful Addresses

**Car seat safety**

Baby Products Association,
Erlegh Manor,
Vicarage Road,
Pitstone, Leighton Buzzard,
Beds LU7 9EY
Tel: 01296 662789

Britax Customer Services department
Tel: 01264 333343

In-Car Safety Centre,
Unit 5, The Auto Centre,
Stacey Bushes,
Milton Keynes
Tel: 01908 220909

Kidscape,
152 Buckingham Palace Road,
London SW1 9TR
Tel: 0171 730 3300

Klippan Help Line
Tel: 01228 35544.

**Food, consumer and environment**

British Union for the Abolition of
  Vivisection,
16A Crane Grove,
London N7 8LB
Tel: 0171 700 4888

Consumer's Association,
Tel: 0171 830 6000

Department of the Environment
Pollution Helpline
Tel: 0800 556677 (calls free)

Food Commission,
3rd Floor,
5-11 Worship Street,
London EC2A 2BH
Tel: 0171 628 7774

Friends of the Earth,
26-28 Underwood Street,
London N1 7JQ
Tel: 0171 490 1555

Greenpeace,
Greenpeace House,
Canonbury Villas,
London N1
Tel: 0171 354 5100

National Federation of City Farms,
The Green House,
Hereford Street, Bedminster
Bristol BS3 4NA
Tel: 0117 923 1800

Women's Environmental Network,
87 Worship Street,
London EC2A 2BE
Tel: 0171 247 3327

**Health**

British Allergy Foundation,
Deepdene House,
30 Bellegrove Road, Welling,
Kent DA16 3BY
Tel: 0181 303 8583

British Homeopathic Association,
27A Devonshire Street,
London W1N 1RJ
Send SAE for list of practitioners

General Council and Register of
  Osteopaths,
56 London Street, Reading,
Berkshire RG1 4SQ
Tel: 01734 576585

Health Education Authority,
Hamilton House,
Mabledon Place,
London WC1H 9TX
Tel: 0171 413 1987

Institute for Complementary Medicine,
PO BOX 194, London SE16 1QZ
Tel: 0171 237 5165

International Association of Infant Massage
London W1P 3PF

London College of Massage,
5 Newman Passage,
London W1P 3PF

National Asthma Campaign,
Providence House,
Providence Place,
London N1 ONT
Tel: 0171 226 2260

National Eczema Society,
Tavistock House East,
Tavistock Square,
London WC1H 9SR
Tel: 0171 388 4097

National Institute of Medical Herbalists,
56 Longbrook Street,
Exeter EX4 6AX
Tel: 01392 426022

National Meningitis Trust,
Fern House,
Bath Road, Stroud,
Gloucestershire GL5 3TJ
Tel: 01453 751738

Osteopathic Centre for Children,
Honeysuckle Cottage,
Inkpen Lane,
Forest Row,
East Sussex RH 18 5BQ
Tel: 01342 824466.

Society of Homoeopaths,
2 Artizan Street,
Northampton NN1 4HU.
Send SAE for register of professional
homoeopaths

**Industry and manufacturers**

Auro,
Saffron Walden,
Essex
Tel: 01709 24744
(Suppliers of organic paints)

British Plastics Federation,
5 Belgrade Square,
London SW11
Tel: 0171 235 9483

Chemical Industries Association,
Kings Buildings,
Smith Square,
London SW1P 3JJ
Tel: 0171 8334 3399

**Pregnancy, birth and babycare**

Association of Breastfeeding Mothers,
26 Hershell Close,
London SE26 4TH
Tel: 0181 778 4769

Baby Milk Action,
23 St Andrew's Street,
Cambridge CB2 3AX.
Tel: 01223 464420

Cot Death Helpline
Tel: 0171 235 1721

Foresight,
The Association for the Promotion of
    Preconceptual Care,
28 The Paddock,
Godalming,
Surrey GU7 1XD
Tel: 01483 4427839

Foundation for the Study of Infant
    Deaths (FSID),
14 Halkin Street,
London SW1X 7DP

Karvol Sleep Clinic Service,
5th Floor, 37 Golden Square,
London W1R 4AH
Send an SAE for details of sleep clinics.

La Leche League of Great Britain,
BM3424,
London WC1N 3XX.
Tel: 0171 242 1278

The Maternity Alliance,
45 Beech Street,
London EC2 P 2LX
Tel: 0171 588 8582

National Association of Nappy Services,
St George House,
Birmingham BS4 AN
Tel: 0121 693 4949

National Childbirth Trust,
Alexandra House,
Oldham terrace, Acton,
London W3 6NH
Tel: 0181 992 8637
NCT branches regularly hold
secondhand clothes sales.

Real Nappy Association
PO BOX 3704,
London SE26 4RX

Toxoplasmosis Trust,
46 Ashburnham Place,
London SE10 8UG
Tel: 0181 692 2599

**Safety**

Child Accident Prevention Tust,
28 Portland Place,
London W1N 4DE
Tel: 0171 636 2545

Royal Society for the Prevention of
    Accidents (RoSPA)
Tel: 0121 200 2461

**Toys**

National Association of Toy and Leisure
Libraries (NATLL),
68, Churchway,
London, NW1 1TL
Tel: 0171 387 9592

# Index